SERRATED

by
Tracy Stombres
and Stephanie Angelo

THANK YOU

I just wanted to thank you, (Grandma) Lillian Calderon, I want to express my appreciation for all your support during the past few years writing this book, and just being a friend during hard times and losing your beautiful daughter, love you very much. God will bless.

To my children, Chelsea and Alex, you guys understand better than most people the difficulties I've been facing with all the good and bad times. I'm very grateful to have two very beautiful kids, thanks so much for giving me some time to write this book.

 With love always,
 Tracy Stombres, Mom

Many thanks to my husband who said "I think you should do it" after I told him I'd been asked to write this book. Ara Dania 'cause you make me laugh. Publishing guru, Jerry Simmons, if there's something about publishing he doesn't know – it simply hasn't been invented. Author Jeff Rivera for being so cool about helping us. Doreen Nicholas for making connections. Mairead Kenny for reading the manuscript. No wonder the word "read" is in your name. I was honored when you read Chelsea's letter to your sons and talked with them about abuse. I hope more parents follow your lead.

 Stephanie Angelo

A portion of the proceeds from this book will be designated towards opening and maintaining Vina's Place Domestic Violence Shelter.

Published by Western Light Publishers, LLC
Tempe, AZ 85284
ISBN 978-0-615-38763-5

No part of this publication may be reproduced, stored in a retrieval system, or transmitted in whole or in part, in any form or by any means, electronic, mechanical, photocopying, recording, or otherwise, without the prior written permission of Tracy Stombres and Stephanie Angelo, Phoenix, Arizona, except for brief quotations in reviews.

Book design and layout by Mullins Creative, Inc., Scottsdale, Arizona
www.MullinsCreative.com

Printed and bound in the United States of America

Copyright © 2010 by Tracy Stombres and Stephanie Angelo.
All rights reserved.

SERRATED

Evidence Item #9: Black handled knife, broken at the handle with a serrated blade. The knife handle and blade both had bloodstains. The knife was discovered inside a sewing kit. It was setting on the bed in the upstairs bedroom, 8'5" east of the west bedroom wall, 8'2" north of the south bedroom wall.

Phoenix Police Department Report Supplement
8/1/2001 DR NO.: 2001 11434625

FOREWORD

My phone rang, jarring me from whatever project I was working on at the time. A woman's voice rushed through, saying, "My name is Tracy and I'm calling you about your book." It took me a second to lock onto what she was talking about. Two weeks earlier I'd gone to the Arizona Coalition Against Domestic Violence and told one of the trainers I was writing a book called, **Battered and Abused – Bringing the Darkness into the Light.** I was looking for survivors who were interested in contributing their stories. Already several women had. Tracy wanted to meet to discuss hers. It was very involved, she said. There was a homicide.

Standing in line at Starbucks, I watched every single woman that walked in the door. Each time I wondered, *"Is that her?"* But one after the other they didn't look as if they were looking for me. One after the other I thought, *Should I approach her? Could that be Tracy?*

When Tracy walked in the door, I knew instantly. It wasn't the way she looked. It was the way we connected. She walked right up to me as if she knew me too.

Looking at Tracy and me, we must seem like unlikely friends. She's tall, dark, exotic, and strikingly beautiful. Her clothes are revealing and sexy. Mine are conservative and probably boring. We're polar opposites. But it took all of about five minutes for me to realize how much alike we really are. And over the course of our friendship and writing process, I have found more and more in common with Tracy. Although, as a private person, I rarely tell her, and there's much more in common than she knows. I still find it amusing when I tell her something about my life that surprises her. Tracy's not easily surprised.

I recorded our first conversation so I could take notes from it. We were sitting on the patio and the mister system was practically raining on us. The recording was total static. Her story was horrific. From the time Tracy was born her life has been difficult and painful. She has endured more than most. I vaguely remembered when her attack was on the news two years prior. I wasn't working in domestic abuse then. Much of what she told me seemed so extreme it was hard to believe. At that point in her life, her former husband was in prison and she was preparing for a civil trial against him which would take place in a year.

Tracy told me she wasn't really looking to meet me to contribute to my book. She wanted me to help her write hers. She wanted to write her life story but knew she couldn't write it. "Absolutely not," I said. "There's no way I'd have the time." Let alone everything else it takes to be co-author of another's life story. We talked a few more minutes and said our goodbyes. After a large iced tea, Tracy made a beeline for the restroom, saying, "I'm dying here!" I couldn't help but be amazed that she was capable of using those words so casually, the way most of us take for granted. There was a time in her life when she really thought, *I'm dying here!*

I got all of three blocks away when I realized I had to write the book. It was something I had to do, and Tracy is a person I felt drawn to work with. I called Tracy a couple days later and said, "I'm in."

During the course of our working together, I experienced parts of the book with her. I knew the attorneys from the Never Again Foundation. I went there on several occasions for many reasons. Tracy's civil trial, a year after we met, was delayed by a couple weeks, preventing me from being there, as I had travel plans that entire summer. But we spoke while I was away. I poured through the newspapers the day I returned. The previous day's paper had the outcome. I read it not knowing yet that Tracy had already left me a voice mail message of the verdict.

During the course of our work together, I listened to the recording of the 9-1-1 tape, watched the news video tapes and the Montel Williams Show appearance. I've spoken to a friend of mine, a lieutenant, who happened to be on the law enforcement team at the scene of the attack. I read reams of court testimony from both the criminal and the civil trials, and read 90 pages of police reports. I viewed 700 police photographs from the attack, now on CDs. Some are so graphic that I would have to walk away from my computer to compose myself. Tracy and I walked around her former home and stood by the fire hydrant where the EMTs left her mother's body.

In writing this book we have laughed, we've cried, and we've shared. Tracy has a lot of friends. I'm glad now to be among them. I remember once when I responded to a comment of hers, she said, "I forgot. You know everything about me. You're the only one who does."

That's a role I don't take lightly. It's been a journey writing this book together. One of many hours and much trust. You'll notice that Tracy's style is narrative and somewhat detached. It's not that she's not emotionally connected to her own story or her life. Quite the opposite. The reality is, though, that people who have survived severe trauma, and who suffer from Post Traumatic Stress Disorder (PTSD) often emotionally disengage themselves just to cope with the pain. It's a form of mental self defense, called Dissociation. That's what you'll find in this book, but it's as much a part of who Tracy is as any other aspect of her personality.

We decided to change several people's names in this story, including Tracy's ex-husband's. The reality is that it doesn't really matter whether individuals like him are identified by name because there are thousands of him "out there."

Tracy's story is an important one. Our goal is that you understand how this can happen to anybody. And how our justice system continues to fail us. The good news is that some things in our legal system have changed since Tracy's attack. But we have a long, long way to go. You can be a part of that change, because it takes all of us to speak up together. Our hope is that this book will mean as much to you to read as it did for us to write.

~ Stephanie

TABLE OF CONTENTS

Chapter One	| Serrated	1
Chapter Two	| Passing Childhood	5
Chapter Three	| Spotlight	17
Chapter Four	| Nesting	23
Chapter Five	| Frank	27
Chapter Six	| Sin City	39
Chapter Seven	| Dead Woman Walking	55
Chapter Eight	| Deadly Awakening	67
Chapter Nine	| Spotlight	73
Chapter Ten	| PTSD	87
Chapter Eleven	| Can You Hear Me?	87
Chapter Twelve	| Court Injustice	107
Chapter Thirteen	| Never Again	137
Epilogue		153
My Hero		157
Are These Things Happening in Your Relationship?		159
References and Resources		161
Suggested Reading		161
About the Authors		163

ONE

SERRATED

I'm drowning. The weight of the water crushes my chest. I can hear the water flooding my ears.

A hollow, echoing sound. But I breathe. Shallow breaths so my chest doesn't move. I can't let it move but I don't remember why.

How can I be breathing if I'm drowning? Slowly I regain my thoughts. I'm not drowning. I'm lying on my mother's bedroom floor. I remember now, the knife slicing through me, coming at me over and over. Legs cut. Arms cut. My hands up. *Keep out of my face!* Out of the corner of my eye, I see my nose hanging to the side. Turning my head over, I throw up.

I remember now. Him. Holding my hair, trying to cut off my head.

I remember now why I can't breathe. If I do, he'll know I'm still alive.

Don't breathe. Don't move. Don't breathe!

I'm trying to think. A million pictures flood my brain. *Alex. Where's Alex? Baby, are you ok? Don't look at Mommy. Don't see me bleed.*

Chelsea. God, if she comes home he'll kill her. *Chels, don't let him see you. Don't see me like this.*

Mom? Where are you?

She got out. I saw. Crawling. Hands and knees. Must have called the police. Hours ago. *Where are they? Why's it taking so long?*

It's sweltering. Arizona's unbearable, stifling summer heat more than 100 degrees. I need water. I've been lying here for so long. If he sees me sweat, he'll know I'm alive.

I'm going to die here. My kids! I can't leave them. I can't leave them to him. I refuse to die. I won't let him win. Not this time! This time, *this time* for sure, they'll put him away for good. It's the one thing that keeps me holding on. He'll be put away for good.

The ringing phone jars my brain. He answers, "Hello?" He listens. "I have a gun," he says. *Who is he talking to? When will someone help me?* He puts the phone close to my head. He says, "Here." I hear a voice I don't recognize. "Are you okay?" it says. I'd give anything to cry for help. If I do he'll get even madder. He'll kill me before help gets here. A sound barely makes it out of me. I have no strength. I whisper painfully. A moan so soft it's a sigh. The voice asks again. *Do they really think I can answer?*

I see spots of light in front of my eyes. *How can he do this to me? I think my mom got out safely. Why isn't anyone helping me?* I think if I could just crawl to that window, I could get out.

He's wandering around the house, pacing. He's on the phone. He says, "I have a gun. And I'll shoot a cop." That's who it is. He's on the phone with the police. I think this will all end soon. I see him putting the broken knife in the box where my mother keeps her sewing supplies. Then he grabs her big silver sewing scissors. *Here we go again,* I think. He shows them to me.

The phone rings. "Mom," he whimpers. "I just stabbed Tracy." He's crying. "I'm scared to go to jail. I'm going to kill myself. I don't want to do life in prison." He listens for a while and then hangs up. The phone rings again. He picks it up. He tells the person on the other end he does not want to surrender. I can tell it's the police again. He says he wants to talk to his brother in Texas. He asks to talk to his mother again.

This is crazy. Will I ever be saved?

Hours have passed. It's getting darker outside. Sweat drips from my head into my mouth. My entire face feels wet and sticky with it. I taste it. It's thick, warm, metallic tasting. This isn't sweat. My blood runs into my mouth.

I hear his heavy steps. Leaning over, he breathes into my face. His breath is hot, claustrophobic, cigarette breath. He kicks my ribs and I hear the crack, and a volt of pain seizes me. He hisses, "Aren't you dead yet, Bitch?"

With every drop of blood, life seeps from my body. *Hold on. Hold on. Don't let him win. Don't let him win!*

Blood fills my ears, I hear only echoes. My thoughts go black and I lose consciousness.

TWO

PASSING CHILDHOOD

Sitting in the back seat of the tiny car, I was hot, uncomfortable, and surrounded by piles of clothes and household belongings. There was barely any room to squeeze me in among the junk, hardly any of which was mine. My mother and her husband were sitting up front. He was a big, hairy, guy with a scraggly beard and questionable hygiene. He smelled funky which amplified the closeness of the tiny car. He didn't like me and I didn't like him. But I was part of the package that came with my mother. We barely talked. I was nervous as hell and scared to death, but I was angry too. I didn't want to live in Arkansas. It seemed like another scheme of my mother's, designed for a happier life. Another man in her life, "This one is different." It was a miserable three-day drive. We left Arizona late at night and didn't stop to rest until the middle of the second day. It was the only stop we made other than quick restroom and food breaks. I was so nervous and depressed. I had really nice acrylic finger nails, but I bit them off one by one on the way to Arkansas as I watched the trees swoosh by. I hunkered down with my Walkman, listening to my favorite band, Rush. *Why is this happening to me?* I wondered.

My father had been an Olympic swimmer and my mother was a hairstylist. Everything was alright until I was two years old, when my dad went to San Luis, Mexico with some friends. According to the stories my mother told me as I was growing up, he'd tried heroin in a motel room and overdosed. He passed out. He was dying. His friends were afraid to call an ambulance or the police. They didn't call anyone. They decided to just let him die. They wrapped him up in the sheets and stuck him in the trunk of a car to die.

A day passed and then one of the four guys called my mom. She "lost it," loaded her gun, and drove all the way to Mexico. I assume now that she was planning on killing the guys that let my dad die. She got to the hotel where the four guys were and pointed the gun at the bunch of them. She was aching to shoot. She was shaking and asking, "Why? Why? You killed my husband!" One of the four guys grabbed her arm, "Calm down, Vina. Just calm down." Eventually she did. She took my dad's body back to Phoenix and had him buried.

My mother coped by self medicating, usually with alcohol and partying. One afternoon she went to the lake with her friends, and as usual, she was drinking. On her way back from the lake, she lost control of her Camaro and rolled it. She crashed through the windshield and crumpled in a heap several feet away. When the ambulance showed up, they declared her dead for three minutes, but they revived her. Her face was cut up and her legs were crushed. They took her to the hospital, gave her a blood transfusion, and performed plastic surgery on her face. After that incident, she would still drink and party constantly. She learned nothing from her near-death experience.

My brother, Glenn, is only ten months younger than I am. When we were toddlers, she left me and my brother in a taxicab at the airport so she could go to Hawaii. She told the cab driver to take us to my grandmother's. We stayed with my grandma for about two months while my mom was in Hawaii. We missed her and didn't understand why she was gone. When she got back, my mother took us to her little apartment that same night, as if nothing had happened.

About a month later, she was out partying again even though my two-year-old brother, Glenn, was sick. My grandmother showed up when my mom was gone and found us alone at the apartment. My brother had a very, very high fever. She took us to the hospital. The emergency room doctor said he could have died.

My grandmother decided to legally take us from my mother. The trial lasted a week before she could get custody of us. Glenn and I had to go on the stand to testify. They would give us a sucker if we told the judge who we wanted live with. My brother and I both said we wanted live with my grandmother, and so my grandparents won full custody.

We were both three years old, and we were happy with my grandmother. She offered love, guidance, and stability—things we'd never had. She had us in dance, ballet, and gymnastics; and she had me in modeling. My grandfather didn't participate much. He was older than my grandmother by several years. Most nights he sat in the living room cleaning his guns or reading.

When I was thirteen, I moved to Texas with my mother and her husband, Larry, and lived in an apartment for awhile. Glenn stayed behind with my grandmother. He had either run away or was in juvenile detention. He was gone so much sometimes I didn't know where he was. I was nervous and scared to death being in a new state, going to a new school, and meeting new people. When I was a girl, I didn't like change and I clung to what was familiar and safe. Desperately shy and insecure, I was so scared that first day because I always had gone to the same school and grew up in the same neighborhood with my grandparents. That morning in Texas, I wanted to jump out of the second-story apartment window. That's the first time I had ever thought of killing myself, but there were many more times I considered it in the years to come.

Glenn finally moved in with us. Just in time to see my mother beat up a few times by the creep she was married to. Then she committed some sort of offense, I'll never know what, but she got herself thrown in jail. Larry split for one of his truck routes and didn't bother to make any arrangements for Glenn and me. It was actually pretty fun for a few weeks, just hanging around the house and ignoring school. Not a soul looked in on us. We ran out of food about the same time the utilities stopped working. It was a hoot though; we'd go to the loading docks of grocery stores and grab whatever we could when no one was looking. Ice cream was our favorite. I'm not sure if we gobbled it down so fast to keep it from melting or to keep ourselves from being caught.

We totally blew it the day we stole the three-wheeler from someone's garage. Maybe we wouldn't have gotten caught if I didn't snag my foot on a tree branch and flip us. We got tossed into the Harris County Youth Village. Living hell. Freaky kids lived in that place. Juvenile murderers, drug addicts, prostitutes, and all around whack jobs. Every time I tried to run away I'd get caught and they tied me to a bed in just my bra and panties.

I don't know any details of whether relatives were looking for us or if they knew my mother was in jail. I don't think the Youth Village staff cared. After about six months, Uncle Don, my dad's brother, found out where we were. He flew from Scottsdale, Arizona to Texas to get us. We had never met him before. He took temporary custody of us and took us out of the Youth Village headed for Scottsdale. As grateful as we were to be out of that place, we were going somewhere new again, to live with someone new—again.

We pulled up to one of the nicest homes we'd ever seen. We each had our own room. But it was real strange living with people we didn't even know. We were enrolled in high school in Scottsdale and I lived with my aunt, uncle, and my cousin. She was a couple years older than me and very popular at the same school. My brother and I were really uncomfortable living there. It was like being a not-so-welcome houseguest. We were even scared to go to the refrigerator to get something to eat.

We lived with them for about a year. My brother started to get into a lot of trouble, not coming home at night, ditching school, and talking back to adults. I had a lot of friends and I was growing to like my life in Scottsdale. Then my mother got out of the jail in Texas.

After a year of my brother getting into trouble, my aunt and uncle wanted us to be with my mother. They'd had enough. My mom was going to come out to Scottsdale, from Texas, to get us. Her plan was to move to Arkansas with Larry and she wanted Glenn and me to go with her. I did not want to leave my school and familiar surroundings again. I had already been to three different high schools. Confused and frustrated, I locked my bedroom door and packed all my stuff in a duffle bag. I hoisted the bag out in front of me, climbed out the bedroom window, and ran to my friend's house. They let me live with them so I could go to school and stay in Scottsdale. I would see my aunt and uncle at the grocery store and at different places in Scottsdale, but they would not say anything. I guess they didn't want to bother with me.

I lived with my friend, her sister, and her mom for nearly four months. Now that Glenn was out of detention, my mother went to get him from my uncle's house in Scottsdale and lived with him in Deer Valley, Arizona. Then she found me and wanted me to live with her. I could not stay with my friend and her mother anymore because her mom was scared, thinking she would get in trouble for letting me live there. I felt badly for my mother, so I packed my things and said goodbye to all my friends. I moved to Deer Valley where I lived with my mother, my brother, and Mom's husband. My friends from Scottsdale would drive all the way to Deer Valley to take me to school in Scottsdale, about twenty miles away. That lasted a couple months until we left for Arkansas. Glenn was back in juvenile detention and that left me alone with my mom and Larry.

An uncle on my father's side picked us up one day and put us on a flight to Scottsdale, Arizona. Living in his gorgeous house wasn't the answer to my prayers that I had hoped. As much as I tried to be invisible his wife despised us; and Glenn couldn't stay out of trouble. "I want you out of here!" she demanded, pointing the way to the door. Apparently I was guilty by association. For the next year I lived with various friends and moved frequently, until of course, when my mom showed up.

We drove for three miserable days until we finally got to Arkansas. I set my Walkman aside as we pulled up to this little white house in the woods. It was a tiny two-bedroom home. The house was frequently cold and had an old-fashioned heater, which we had to repeatedly light with a match. This was nothing like my home in Scottsdale. My small room had two windows. The windows faced the woods; all you could see was the woods outside—forever.

The first two weeks we were there, I laid around in a daze. I was really depressed and just listened to my music and missed all my friends. Nothing could pull me out of the funk I was in. I went to a local school and hated it. A couple years later, I began dating this guy, Greg, who lived on the other side of the street. I was sixteen, and he was twenty-one.

My mother constantly went out drinking and when she got home, she would get beat up by her husband. If I got involved or tried to stop it, he would hit me. Once he punched me so hard, I flew into the closet. He called me a bitch and spit on me. I called the police so many times, but they would do nothing. The police would say they didn't see it so they couldn't do anything. "So, does she have to be dead before you do anything?" The police officer pretty much said yes.

One summer night my mom came home drunk. When Larry heard the cab pull up, he ran from the house and grabbed her from the cab by her hair and punched her a couple times. The next morning there was blood all over the shower. After he dragged her all the way into the house, he took her into the bathroom and hit her over and over again. I stayed in my room. I knew he had a lot of guns and I was scared he would use one. I wanted to help her, to scare him with his own gun and make him stop, but I felt powerless. *Would I help or make it worse?*

Eventually I got a little puppy. It was a sad little thing, about six months old and kind of sick. He was always ready to lick my face and to curl up nearby. Larry decided he was going to put my puppy out of his misery, so he went into his storage shed and got a hammer. He started killing my puppy, beating him in the head with the hammer. The puppy was wailing. The sound was horrible. I was screaming at Larry, crying, and begging him to stop. When the puppy was dead, Larry shrugged and walked away. When I was really depressed which was frequently, I would go into the back yard and sit by the puppy's grave, talking to the puppy.

One night my mom went out to party with friends and it got really late, so I was worried. I was seventeen and had just bought a car after saving my money for a long time. Much of the savings had come from the $500 a month I got from Social Security from my dad's death. I drove around looking for my Mom. I went down Main Street in Pine Bluff, Arkansas. It was a very small town and easy to cruise all of it. I finally saw my mom and I told her to get in the car. She was walking alone and said, "No," and I begged, "Please, please get in the car!" Ignoring me, she kept walking. I watched as four guys pulled up next to her in a Cadillac and she got in the car with them. I followed for a while until I lost them, so I just went home. I couldn't sleep all night. The next morning she was still not home. Finally, we got a call from the police, and she was in jail. The cops found her in the park. She had been gang raped by the four guys. But when the police picked her up they found out she had an outstanding warrant held from her arrest for a DUI, so they took her to jail. To them, that was more important than prosecuting a gang rape.

I was living with my stepfather, Larry. From time to time he'd ask me about my friend who'd been raped by her own father. "Did they prosecute the guy?" "Do you think they believed your friend's story?" The innuendo was clear and I was scared to death and completely creeped out. My boyfriend, Greg, said I could stay with him and his family. After a while, Larry went to jail, for what, I don't know. They took him to New York, where he was from, and my mom was expedited to Texas because she was wanted there for the outstanding DUI.

After a while, my mom got out of prison in Texas, came back to Arkansas, and got her hairdressing job back. We first got a little apartment together and then she met another guy and we ended up moving in with him in his trailer. My mom hadn't changed her drinking and partying ways at all.

On a weekend trip to the lake, we met a lot of guys. My mom ended up leaving with one and I went home. She never showed up all night, and my mom's new boyfriend, Terry, asked me where she was. "I don't know. We were at the lake and she left with someone." The next morning, I was at the breakfast table quietly eating watermelon and trying not to wake Terry, when my mother showed up with a new man I recognized from the lake. In a flash, Terry jerked out of bed and grabbed his shotgun. He bolted outside, shooting his gun wildly, and shot holes all along the side of the man's car. Terry took off running. My mom ran into the house screaming at me to get something to tie around this guy's leg. I ran in my closet and grabbed a belt to tie around his leg. His leg was blown almost all the way off. It was just hanging there pumping out blood. We carried him to the passenger side of the car and my mom told me to drive. I drove all the way to the hospital doing about 100 miles per hour. They said they were going to keep him there for a couple weeks. He gave us his car keys and his wallet. We used his credit card for food and hotel. We were scared to go back to the trailer. Law enforcement was looking everywhere for my mom's boyfriend and we did not want to go home right away. When we finally had the courage to go back, the scene looked bad, really bad. There were bullet holes all over the car. My mom's boyfriend's things were still in the trailer. The watermelon I'd been eating was still on the table and ants were crawling all over it.

Somehow my mother got fired from her hairdresser job. We didn't have money to eat so we stole eggs from the neighbor's chicken coop. Not having any money to eat didn't stop my mother from drinking though. Her next DUI earned her two years in jail.

The owner of the trailer wouldn't let me stay there. I didn't have any money, and I mean none. I had my car and all I did was drive and cry, cry and drive. Like being on auto-pilot I turned into the parking lot of a pool hall I'd been to before. The owner let me use the phone to call long distance. One of the only numbers I knew was my mother's brother, Uncle Richard, in California. I told him I had nowhere to go. I was homeless and hungry. I heard the smirk in his voice, "Oh well, life's a bitch."

Next I tried my grandparents and my grandfather answered the phone. When I told him what was going on, he hung up on me. I tried again and he hung up. Twice, three times. How did this get to be my fault? I didn't know what to do. "Listen girl, said the bar owner, "I'll pay for two weeks for you and the hotel and here's fifty for food. But that's it. Two weeks" "Oh my God! Thank you!"

But those two weeks seemed like two minutes and after they were up I lived in my car; where two minutes seems like two weeks.
It rains in Arkansas practically every day. My car's windows leaked, so I was always wet and wore smelly, mildewed clothes. I parked my car and slept at the truck stop a couple days. "Jinx," a long

haul driver, was about the age my dad would have been if he'd been alive, brought me food and money in exchange for helping him wash the diesel trucks. After about a week, he asked me if I wanted to go with him on a truck route. I said yes. Heck, I had nothing else to do and nowhere else to go. The first route took us to California, with a detour to Arizona. I hadn't seen my grandparents in a couple of years. I asked my grandmother if she had any clothes, or tee shirts, or anything I could have, but she said no. She gave me all my roller skating trophies and some of my things. I was hoping my grandmother would ask me to stay with her. She handed me my things; hugged me goodbye and shut the door.

Jinx introduced me to the drug that helped the drivers stay awake—crank. I would watch daylight go down and daylight come up. I would never sleep. I wouldn't eat. He would try to force me to eat. I had no interest in food and became rail thin. We drove everywhere. After we left California we had to go to Utah and then on to Saint Louis, Chicago, through Virginia, Detroit, and Canada. I was so out of it, I couldn't keep track of where we were. I didn't care. Jinx called me his "spare daughter." I was seventeen and he was forty-seven. He took pretty good care of me except the drugs, which we both used heavily. We would go to truck stops to sleep—well, rest—because I didn't actually sleep much. There would be prostitutes there. All the truck drivers would ask Jinx, "Who is that pretty girl with you?" But Jinx would never hurt me and he never tried to have sex with me, but all the weird truckers scared me.

We had to go to Canada, but we went through Detroit first. Small homeless children were everywhere—at the bus stops and along the streets. It was a very sad city from what I could see. Looking down from the high windows of the eighteen-wheeler, I thought, "Are these kids really so different from me? Where will they end up?"

We were approaching the Canadian border after what seemed like an eternity. Jinx put his gun and drugs down a fiberglass hole in the truck to hide them. When the Canadian border control asked us if we had any weapons, we said no. They asked how old I was and I said eighteen. They asked who the guy was. I said, "My stepfather." That didn't do it for them and they were suspicious. They ordered us out of the truck and searched it. They found the gun. Border control handcuffed us while other truckers gawked and inwardly breathed sighs of relief. We spent the night in a Canadian jail. I was separated from Jinx. We were in another country, I was in trouble, and I was scared. *Please don't let this be like Harris County again!* They kept us overnight and confiscated the gun. They let us finish our truck route in Canada. Jinx bought me a Greyhound ticket to Arkansas and I headed back alone.

THREE

SPOTLIGHT

Back in Arkansas I walked to my ex-boyfriend Greg's house from the bus terminal. He was living with his parents again. At night, Greg would open the back door and together we'd tiptoe into the kitchen so I could eat while his parents slept.

He would take me to my car every now and then so I could get clothes. We'd go to Laundromats or, if I was lucky, sneak to his parents' house to wash my clothes. We hung out at his friend's house, or at his uncle's. His uncle was a drug dealer. Everyone sat around shooting heroin up their arms. I had a natural affinity for hypodermic needles. I became the "injectionist" of choice, something about measuring the drug and pushing the plunger appealed to me.

Jinx finally came back. It was a relief to see him hanging around the truck stop. He gave me his Blazer to drive around and decided to have me find a place for us to live together. "Us" being Jinx, myself, and Jinx's son, "Blue Boy." Blue Boy was younger than me by a few years.

I was incredibly happy. I drove around looking at apartments, listening to music, and reveling in the knowledge that I would have a place to live and a room of my own. *At last!*

It was a party hang-out. Day in and day out—it wasn't normal the novelty wore off and I felt like my life was going nowhere. I knew the only way to leave the drug-induced life was to leave Arkansas and everything with it. I needed to get out.

When Jinx and Blue Boy weren't home, I packed my few things; mostly clothes and skating trophies. Whatever I could fit in one little suitcase. I had no choice but to leave some clothes and my car behind. Then I just left. It's not that I didn't care for them, but I was sure if I told them, they would have tried to talk me out of it. I needed a clean break if I was going to get away from a life of drugs.

I was going back to Phoenix to live with an uncle, someone Glenn had found. On the day of my flight, I called Greg to take me to the airport. I never told Jinx and Blue Boy I was going. Greg cried and cried that I was leaving.

I barely knew these new people I was going to live with. **Haven't I done this before?** Off the airplane in Phoenix, I searched the faces for one that might be familiar. He'd described himself as tall and bald. Found him! My uncle Dick, from my Dad's side. He and his wife took me to their apartment and gave me a room. They later let me fix it up the way I liked. But that first night back I felt really sick, cramping, and in pain. I was bleeding badly and had no idea why. My aunt took me to the hospital. I was having a miscarriage. I didn't even know I was pregnant. The nurse thought it had something to do with the flight. She chalked it up to "just not meant to be." Really it could have been drugs, stress, anything. Sometimes you never know why.

My aunt was a clean freak and compulsive about perfection. She and my uncle had both been in the military and maybe it had never left her system. She was incredibly strict with me. Even at eighteen I had a ten o'clock curfew. I respected it, but I also had a lot of friends and felt I had no life. Not so easy a transition for a girl that had years of unrestricted freedom.

Chapter Three | Spotlight

She didn't like me and didn't want me in the house. According to my uncle, it wasn't working out. They offered to help me find a studio apartment, but I would have to start working to pay my rent. We found a second-story studio apartment. My uncle paid the moving costs, gave me start-up rent and grocery money, and that was that.

Next to a dumpster, I found the world's ugliest couch, but back then, I thought it was nice. Isn't there a saying about one man's trash being another one's treasure? I collected crates for my tables and fixed up my new place the best I could.

For the first time things were working out nicely for me. There was a plaza a few blocks from my apartment where I got a job as a "Salad Girl" at the Sizzler restaurant. After a few weeks I took a second job at a bagel shop a few doors from Sizzler. A few weeks later the plaza's Hollywood Video rental hired me too.

Zip, zip, zip, I would go from one business to the next sometimes working all three jobs and sixteen hours a day. I needed a large purse to carry my three uniforms! If I had a day off at one job, I worked two of the others. I never had a day where I wasn't working somewhere.

After three months, I finally had enough saved to buy a cute, baby blue Honda Prelude. It was used, but it was mine. I could barely afford the $300 a month payment and insurance. Now that I had wheels, I was ready to look for a better-paying job.

Close to my apartment was a bar advertising for waitresses. I spoke to the manager, and now, at nineteen, I was old enough to work there—even though I wasn't old enough to drink. The manager asked me to come for an interview at eleven the next morning.

Sitting there waiting to speak to him, I saw all these beautiful girls coming out of a back room wearing little bikinis—some even wore no tops at all. *Oh, my God! What is this?* I never saw anything like this in Arkansas! "This is a topless bar," said the manager, "and if you want to work here as a waitress you can make a lot of money." *Done!* I thought, filled out the application, and asked him what to wear. "Any kind of bathing suit." I was to start the next night and spent the entire day looking for a nice bathing suit.

As awkward as I felt wearing a swimsuit, I took to it right away and found it comfortable and natural to talk to customers. I did it for the tips. They came easily and that's what mattered.

Not a year went by before the manager asked me to dance and strip at the bar. "No way!" I was shy, scared, and had no idea how I'd do something like that. It was OK for the other girls if that's what they wanted to do for a living. *But me? Dance? Topless?* I couldn't imagine it. All the girls kept telling me about the money I'd make, and how easy it was once you get started. The idea of the money was so enticing. Maybe I just wouldn't have to struggle so much. And these girls were nice; it wasn't like they were so different from any other girls my age. *Would it really be so bad?*
Once up there on stage, I closed my eyes and pretended I was at a night club with friends. I just let the music envelop me and blocked everyone and everything out of my mind. I let my mind wander with the beat of the music, closed my eyes for a moment and felt some sort of release within myself. With a whistle here and a gesture there, the patrons flagged me over for tips. Money was all over the stage and it was intoxicating.

Life was great. At almost twenty years old, I was finally enjoying each day. For a time I stayed in the studio apartment with my dumpster furniture. But I could afford to buy little things. I danced Thursday, Friday, and Saturday and started to enjoy days off. I was able to quit my three other jobs. I would drive around looking at furniture for "someday." I'd spent my entire life being poor and it was finally turning around.

I was anxious to get out of the neighborhood I was in. It was a popular place for drug peddling and child predators. Crime was everywhere.

I got another apartment down the street. I'd only been there a short while when one early morning I got home from the strip club and found my apartment had been ransacked. Someone had broken in and stolen the things I'd worked so hard for and tore my whole closet apart looking for money. I called the police and they came and took fingerprints. I found out the people who broke in climbed three balconies up from the ground level and got in through my Arcadia door. They'd stolen a lot from me and I decided to move again. It seemed like I was moving every three to six months. It paid off. Emotionally I was freer than I'd ever been. Financially I was comfortable and didn't want for anything.

I found a really nice one-bedroom apartment above one of the popular resorts in Phoenix. The apartment building was huge with mountain views, security guards, and waterfalls that I could hear from my bedroom window as I slept at night. It was so peaceful. I bought all new furniture, including a nice white sectional, and had it delivered to me. Pointing to this corner and that, I told the delivery guys where to set my things. What fun!

The resort had a restaurant and a pool on top of the mountain. When I sat in the Jacuzzi, I could see the whole city. They served drinks while I sunbathed. I was loving life! I continued to work at the strip club and make lots of money. I started drinking a lot at the resort's restaurant bar. I'd have a good buzz on before going to work. My mom started to come around, visiting and spending the night. Then my brother needed a place to live for a while so I let him stay with me. When I went to work, he would have big parties and bring girls to my apartment. I was so pissed off! When I got back, my place was a mess and things would be missing, so I told him he needed to go.

SERRATED

My mom would bring biker guys over to the pool. They brought a lot of beer and made rowdy noise. That kind of stuff was sure not allowed at this high-dollar resort, so a few days later, the landlord told me that I needed to keep my mom away or get out.

I ended up leaving. I gave up my apartment so I could stick with my family.

Four

NESTING

As kids living with our grandmother, Glenn and I were put into a variety of activities. We danced and roller-skated for about three years. Glenn was a really good skater. It was a huge commitment for our grandmother. She poured a lot of money into these activities and committed to waking up at four in the morning to get us to competitions. Many of the competitions were within Arizona, but a lot were out of state. To compete, we needed nice costumes, which was another huge expense for my grandmother. I got first place a lot. It was fun and hard work.

My grandmother also put me into modeling. I did both runway and commercial work. This was the hardest for me, being as shy and insecure as I was which is exactly why my grandmother did it. She knew we needed something to help us feel better about ourselves and develop our sense of self-esteem. As a child, I felt different from all the other girls. They lived with fathers and mothers. They had parents that came to competitions and cheered from the stands. To be living with your grandparents was an oddity to them.

By the time I was stripping at twenty, I found myself back in modeling. At the club, guys would approach me and ask me to meet them for different modeling jobs, but I didn't trust anyone.

After a while the same man and woman kept showing up at my work all the time. It was like they were watching me and checking me out. Eventually they asked me to model for them in a house in Scottsdale. They said they were in Phoenix from London and would pay me $500 a day for a few days to do swimwear and lingerie modeling. I set up an appointment to meet with them and went to the house in Scottsdale. It was beautiful. It was of typical southwest style with vaulted ceilings and Saltillo tile. A lot of "coin" went into that place.

Impressed and enticed by the money, I signed a release to work with them. They told me to be back early the next morning for a day-long shoot. We did bikini and lingerie photographs. We did a few shots in the pool and several in the house, all over the property. I had a makeup artist and a hairdresser. For a girl who'd never been pampered, it was a treat. It was fun, clean, and they were nice to me. I was going to be in a London-based magazine. The couple paid me for five days' work. Twenty-five hundred dollars!

I continued to dance at the club and then another guy came in and wanted me for swimwear modeling. I made some money at that. After that, another man came in and wanted me to go to Hollywood and pose in *Hustler* magazine. I ended up posing for another magazine called *Swank*.

I said I wasn't sure about that one, so I got his card. He said they would pay me a thousand dollars, but I would have to go to Hollywood for a while. I wanted to think about it. The money was really tempting and I'd never been to Hollywood. I hadn't been back to California since I was a toddler. I called him and told him I was ready to do it. He arranged for me to fly out there. I was so nervous! I didn't know if this guy was crazy or lying. Could I trust him? "Sometimes you have to take chances in life or you will always be in the same situation," I assured myself.

When I arrived in Los Angeles, I talked to him non-stop

in the car, trying to figure him out. "We're there," he said. Parking in a lot, we walked down the street to the studio. We were in the heart of the Hollywood clothing district—there were clothing and lingerie stores everywhere.

He asked me what styles I liked and we bought the wardrobe he thought I needed for the shoot. He selected all kinds of lingerie, boots, and sexy clothes. It was the kind of shopping trip I could only dream of. Then we walked farther down the street, turned down a block, and went into a back door. We entered a huge studio. It was the first time I'd seen anything like it. It was really neat. There were light fixtures everywhere, on stands and hanging from the ceiling. Cameras were set up in different corners. There was furniture for every possible room in a house, artificial plants, and an assortment of artwork.

He told me what to put on and began to set up the Asian background scene for the magazine. He had me put on a red oriental leather outfit. Once I'd changed and came out of the bathroom, he told me to lie on the couch and he started taking pictures. He would tell me which way to lie and when to turn around or what to do. It was pretty easy and I wasn't new at it. Then he told me to take off my top. So I did. I'd modeled before and I'd stripped before, but I was still a little apprehensive about this guy. We were alone, after all.

After he told me to put my top back on, he continued to take pictures. He had me take off my bottoms. *"Oh, God,"* I thought as I did it. I was still only twenty and a few thousand dollars was a lot to me, especially after being homeless, more than once, and having three jobs at the same time just to survive. I liked the idea of making a few thousand!

He took pictures for about two hours. After I got dressed, he had me sign a model release. He said my pictures would be in *Swank* magazine or *Hustler*. We needed to wrap up, he said, there was going to be a crew of people coming to the studio any minute to film a porno flick. Would I be willing to be in it? "Oh, no way!" "OK" he said, "you can just watch before your flight leaves in a couple hours."

This felt like a moment of truth for me. I struggled with "need" over "want." I *need* more money. I *need* more independence. This was one area where as hard as it was to walk away from the money I knew I'd have to look myself in the eyes every day. What I didn't want was to sink to a new low.

Almost immediately, all the crew people for the porno movie came into the studio. I sat there and watched them put it together, talking about the scenes. Then I watched them shoot the porno movie. OK, I've had weird experiences. This was bizarre! How do you watch people have sex on cue? "No, stop here"; "Put your hand like this"; "We need to change this light there." My photographer was telling me that they are all clean and they get checked for STDs weekly. "Think about it, Tracy. You could make a couple thousand a day if you wanted to."

I shook my head, "Well, if I was to ever do this, no one would ever want to marry me." He said there are a few porn stars who are married to rich, successful actors. He mentioned Traci Lords, one of the most renowned porn stars of all. He told me what model car she drives and about her beach house and all the "good" things about the job. I said, "No that's OK." So I watched them shoot the film, and afterwards I met everyone on the set.

The photographer knew I was dating someone, and offered my boyfriend $500 to screw me for a porno flick. I'd only casually dated the guy for six months and he actually thought it was a great idea! He begged me to do it. Wasn't the $1000 a day worth it? I was disgusted with him, and with the idea of it.

Five

FRANK

I broke up with the porno-eager boyfriend and moved into a really nice apartment with a spiral staircase leading to an upper loft. There was one guy I would see from time to time in the parking lot of our apartment building. Eventually, he introduced himself and we got to talking. He invited me to a party later that night and I agreed to go with him. After that we saw each other every day. He seemed secure and grounded. He had a steady job working for his parents' company in Phoenix. I had a good job, my life was stable, and our relationship was growing.

In a few months time I discovered I was pregnant and I really wanted this baby. I was twenty-two and after the miscarriage as a teen, I wanted to be sure to keep this baby and have the family of my own I'd never had. This was a baby to love, to call my own, someone who really needed me.

My boyfriend and I moved into a beautiful townhouse together and set up a home. I changed my shift so that I would only work during the day. Once my pregnancy began to show, I couldn't dance anymore and quit my job. My boyfriend agreed to support me and help me go to school. This was a really exciting time in my life. I wanted the "real thing". I wanted everything I'd never had as a kid. I'd never known stability, or a normal, traditional family life. I was aching to give my child the very thing that had lacked in my own life that had made each day painful and awkward. Most of all, I wanted this baby to have a better life than I ever had.

I went to technical school to become a medical assistant. At twenty-three I gave birth to a beautiful and healthy baby girl that we named Chelsea. For the next year our lives were good.

My boyfriend wasn't paying the bills. I'd find unpaid invoices lying around the house and under stacks of papers. The electricity was shut off. In the dark and sweating from lack of air-conditioning, "What the hell is going on and what are you doing with the money?" He refused to answer me. Shrugging me off defiantly he'd strut away. Night after night he'd stay out late. He'd avoid Chelsea and me.

Meth is an all-consuming drug. Once you're on it, nothing and no one will be more important than the high. He refused to quit and refused to get help. I called for a U-Haul and moved Chelsea and myself out. My mother helped me pack and we made the move while my boyfriend was out partying. Not having a place to live yet, I put everything except the essentials into storage and Chelsea and I moved into a motel. My mother was living at my grandparents' house, and while I worked she would care for Chelsea at their place or my motel.

The flea-bag motel was the best I could do. It was costing me forty bucks a night. We were there for six months. Having had my credit ruined by my boyfriend, I couldn't get an apartment anywhere and I was completely broke.

Sometimes I would walk Chelsea down the street to a convenience store for chips and drinks. I ran into a friend from the weekly apartments next door who suggested I meet his new roommate. I wasn't interested. I needed to get my life in order and somewhere better for Chelsea and me to live.

Chapter Five | Frank

After work one night, I found a note stuck in my motel room door. "Frank" it read, with a phone number. Ah, must be my friend's roommate. *Sheesh!* I thought and threw it away. Another night he left his number again. *Oh, what the heck.* I thought and called the number. There's a party, he said. Did I want to go?

Frank and I hung out all night. I thought he was charming, charismatic, and very good-looking. He said and did all the right things. I'd wanted to feel loved and valued for so long. I'd wanted to feel beautiful in a respected relationship, not just as an object for strangers' eyes. Frank was exactly what my life was missing.

I finally moved into an apartment with Chelsea. Frank and I were dating, and after six months, I asked him what he was paying for rent at the weekly apartment. When he told me $200 a week, I suggested he give me the money and move in with my daughter and me.

We were completely in love. He was good towards my daughter.

At one point, Frank told me he was due back in his home state of Texas for a couple months to finish a period of probation. He explained it was a bar fight he'd been in here in Phoenix but the probation was in Texas because his family was there. He was only in Phoenix to finish technical school for electronics. I accepted the explanation, but something didn't feel right..

He called every day from Texas, and then offered to pay for Chelsea and me to come see him. Occasionally, he flew to Phoenix to visit over the weekend. Each time we were separated, I missed him so much.

On January 3, 1996, the day before my birthday, we were married in Texas. His family was happy for us and I was excited. I believed in marriage and commitment—till death do us part.

Back in Phoenix, with Frank still in Texas, the nagging feeling wouldn't go away and I decided to look up public records to find out a little more about his history. I was curious about the bar fight. But the arrest record was all about Frank pulling a knife on a girl. It read that he'd held a knife to her chest and knocked her unconscious. When she awoke, it said, her pants were pulled down.

I called Frank and asked for an explanation. "It's all a lie," he told me. "She caught me cheating on her at my house and pulled a knife from the drawer and tried to stab me, Tracy. But later she told the police she'd lied. I'd pushed her out of the house and told her to never, ever pull a knife on me again."

When I didn't believe Frank, he put his mother on the phone to confirm the story. I was thoroughly confused. The court record showed the girlfriend had recanted her story. Whom do I believe? The mother who wasn't there? My mind bounced from each of the three possible stories. I wanted to know why Frank had used the bar fight story. His mother defended Frank, telling me, "He was afraid you'd think differently of him."

I needed a few days to digest this. He called me every day leaving loving messages that I wouldn't return. I had a new husband I wasn't sure I could trust. I trusted his mother, though, I had no reason not to, and eventually decided to talk to him and let it go. The ex-girlfriend, I figured, must have been a real piece of work. The Frank I knew was gentle and loving, and I couldn't imagine him doing something so vicious. Certainly not to a woman. It gnawed at me though. ***Why hadn't he told me the truth in the first place?***

When Frank got home, things were great. He got a construction job and was promoted to foreman within a month. He worked hard. I still danced, though not as often. Frank wasn't crazy about my job, but he couldn't complain about the income it brought.

Frank and I had gone on a "date night" one night, leaving Chelsea with my mother to have some time alone. We went for drinks at a favorite bar. While we were there, I was not allowed to talk to anyone or he would get really angry and lash out accusations. If

Chapter Five | Frank

I even looked at anyone, he would get mad. This behavior had begun to happen a lot. It wasn't fun going out with him anymore.

When we argued at home, sometimes the police would show up at the house after neighbors complained about the noise. To outsiders, I was anti-social, and having come a long way from the insecurities of my childhood, it's not the impression I wanted to make. For Frank's benefit, I always kept my eyes down and was careful of how I talked, walked, and acted in public. He was always so jealous. We stayed at the bar for a while till his jealousy erupted into a fight. We fought more in the car on our way home. He started acting crazy, like he was going to hit me. This scene was getting all too familiar.

I wanted to leave the bar before we made a public scene. I was driving, Frank was getting ugly, and I was scared. I pulled into a gas station and stopped. Frank kicked the gear shift over and over until it bent out of place. I ran out of the car into the store and told the cashier to call the police.

The police showed up pretty quickly that time. When Frank saw the cops, he took off running and the police gave chase. Then they sent a helicopter to look for him. It circled over the neighborhood, shining its light into backyards and alleys. After about an hour, the helicopter's spotlight found Frank in an empty lot. Officers tackled him and called for backup to the field where they caught him. They put him, handcuffed, into the patrol car and drove him back to the gas station to write the report and talk to the other officers.

Finally, caught in the act, Frank went ballistic and kicked out the window of the cruiser's back seat. The glass broke and a piece flew into an officer's forehead, cutting him. They tackled Frank again and put him into another car and immediately took him to jail.

After that the officers said Frank would have four charges against him. He'd be charged with criminal damages for the gear shift in my car, criminal damage on the officer's car, aggravated assault against the police officer because of the injury, and for resisting arrest.

He spent the night in jail. Surprisingly, he was in a good mood when I picked him up. He just kept asking me, over and over, if he goes to prison for the charges, would I wait for him?

That was a serious question and something I really needed to think about. I told him that I needed to wait and see what was going to happen. He was so scared because he hurt a cop and that, to him, was big. That seemed to have more of an effect on him than anything he'd done to me. It would take a long time for me to realize how significant that was.

Two weeks later, Frank had his first court appearance. They summed up the events of the charges and told him what kind of jail time he was looking at—about seven years for all the offenses. *Seriously?* There was no way I would wait for him for seven years. They set another court date and our lawyer said they would probably plea bargain with him.

As we waited for the next court date, both of us were scared. Had it really come to this? Seven years seemed like a long time in prison. As he predicted, Frank's lawyer said they were offering a plea bargain and it was for two years in prison. Frank gave up one count of criminal damages and settled for two years instead of twelve to fifteen years if he'd gone to trial. We talked about it outside and he asked me if I'd wait two years. Frank was emotional and scared. His question was hard to answer. But by serving the two years with the plea bargain, we didn't risk trial, where he couldn't predict the outcome.

He said if I didn't promise to wait, he'd take off right then. He said no matter what it took, he'd run. He pushed the right emotional buttons and I felt guilty.

He was my husband and I thought I was supposed to be there for him so I said yes. Satisfied, Frank went back inside and set a date to turn himself in, giving us time to get things together before he left. They gave us a couple weeks to get situated at home.

We were both scared. When the date came, he turned himself in and I went home alone. A couple days later, I got a letter from Frank. He wrote every other day and called all the time. He was still controlling, even from prison. Not being able to keep an eye on me, he asked questions in his letters and made comments about what he imagined I was doing. I thought a couple times that I should just divorce him while he was in there. I was now a single working mom to Chelsea, stressed out, and started to drink a lot. I was depressed. I was giving up.

My husband was in prison for aggravated assault against an officer. I was raising my daughter and I was waiting for him to get out of jail. As promised, I was faithful the whole time he was in prison. He was released after a year and a half. He would call me all the time. I was dancing at the topless bar, where I'd been working since I was nineteen. My mom would watch my daughter while I went to work. I was self-medicating with alcohol to escape the sadness in my life.

One night after work, I sat and drank with my boss and a couple girls. One of the other dancers said she needed a ride home so I took her to her apartment complex. I got out of the car and walked her halfway to the door so we could talk a couple more minutes.

As I was walking back to my car, three Native American guys approached me, surrounded me, and asked how I was. They followed me to my car, asking me my name and calling me "baby". The parking lot was badly lit and no one was around. I got in my car and started to back away as fast as I could, but they were behind my car. I was afraid I'd run one over.

Angry now, they grabbed onto my car and wouldn't let go. I decided to fly over the speed bump to throw them off. Maybe that would get rid of them! But they were still hanging on. In a flash of defiant boldness, I stopped and got out and pushed them off my car. I wasn't thinking about what I was risking. I told them to leave me alone. They pushed me on the ground and lifted up my skirt. I thought they were going to rape me. Then they ripped off the license plate from my car and broke it in half. I guessed they were going to steal my car. One of the guys looked in my back seat and saw my makeup bag. He opened it and saw all the tips that I made that night. He grabbed the cash and one of the guys said, "Let her go. Let's get out of here." As soon as they left running, I got up and got back in my car. Shaken, driving down the road, I saw a police officer.

I figured I would do the right thing, so I pulled over to the police car. I was crying and telling them that three guys just stole my money. One officer asked me if I'd been drinking. I told him yes. The cop and his partner told me to put my hands behind my back and they gave me a ticket for driving without a license plate. I told the police that the guys ripped it right in half. The police gave me a ticket for drinking and driving. I asked the cops, "Aren't you guys going to get my money?" They didn't care about helping me. The three guys were just a block away! Instead, the officers put me in the cop car and took me to jail.

I imagined the time when I was a girl living in Texas and my mother was gang raped. When the police found her, she was thrown in jail because she'd been drinking. The rapists were never held accountable. My mother suffered more for being in the wrong place at the wrong time. I pictured being next.

By this time, I was cursing at them while I was going to jail. I asked them, "You'd rather mess with me because I'm a woman and you're scared to go after those guys?"

The police charged me with a DUI. I'd only had one shot of Tequila and barely had a buzz, but they smelled the liquor on my breath. I was asking for help from the guys and getting angry and vocal because the police wouldn't help. They put me in jail without a field sobriety test. A night in jail was my payback for trying to do the right thing. It was a slap in the face for honesty. That was one of the hardest nights of my life. Weeks later, I went to court and told them I was not guilty, because the cops did not "Protect and Serve." They set another court date for a couple weeks later. When I went to court again, they dismissed all the charges. It was a huge, huge relief.

I couldn't wait to pick Frank up on his release date. He looked so good. I'd missed him so much. It was the happiest day of my life besides having my daughter. We settled back into living our lives and talked about making our family of three a family of four and having a baby of our own.

It didn't take long to conceive. Never had. I joked that I could look at a guy's underpants and get pregnant. But Frank started to stay out late and became indifferent to Chelsea and me. I was hormonal, isolated, and depressed. Frank wouldn't answer his cell phone or his pager.

We argued often. His behavior was unpredictable and getting crazier. I was scared of him. I wouldn't hit him or throw anything at him, but I didn't want to be treated that way. After one fight, I went outside to calm down and he locked me out. I was pregnant and my emotions were like a roller coaster. I sat down thinking he'd let me back in. I kept knocking and ringing the doorbell. I yelled through the window asking for the car keys. I wanted to go to my mother's house. He wouldn't do it. I told him I would throw a rock at the car. He still wouldn't let me in. I threw a rock at my windshield. Then Frank called the cops. When they came they said I was going to be charged with criminal damage. I asked them why since it was my car and they said it was community property—belonging to both of us. Plus, they told me, "You have a warrant out for your arrest." They said it was for the DUI I'd gotten three years earlier the night the guys tried to steal my money. I explained it had been dismissed. They said they brought it back up. Apparently, the courts have seven years to do that if they feel like it. I said, "Yeah, soon as I'm pregnant and married they're going to bring stuff back up on me." I went to jail and had to spend the night on the hard floor. I was miserable. It was like my life was getting worse and worse each year. I got out the next day. Frank picked me up and said he felt bad. The police set a court date for the outstanding DUI.

I went to court for the single count DUI and the judge said it was two counts. "Why?" I asked, shocked. The judge said, "One for blowing over the legal limit and one for driving." I couldn't believe it. I was getting a DUI for driving to the police for help.

I was looking at the maximum, six months in jail. But they would plea bargain with me and give me a lesser charge if I would sign "guilty" of one count of endangerment and one count of DUI. "Endangerment—who did I endanger?" They said I had endangered myself. What a concept! "OK, if I sign this plea bargain, what will I get?" I would get four months in jail. Plus for the next three years I would be on probation and my driver's license revoked.

"I'm eight months pregnant right now!" I told them. The judge would let me have my baby first, and then I was expected to turn myself in. In jail, I would get "two for one" so I would only have to do two months.

With a bulging stomach, I couldn't dance. Frank always used our new car and left me stuck at the apartment. He gave me no access to money. While he partied with friends, I cried myself to sleep in Chelsea's room, cuddling my little girl.

My freedom, independence, and access to resources evaporated. I became isolated from friends, family, and the outside world. I was sure Frank was cheating on me. I believed in marriage and now depended on him for food, insurance, housing, and everyday necessities. I had Chelsea to think about and a baby on the way.

Desperately, I called a crisis hotline one night, just for someone to talk to. They sent a representative out at three in the morning who just sat and listened to me. After a while, I felt better.

When I went into labor, Frank was there. Alexander was a healthy ten pound baby. Frank was ecstatic. His attitude and devotion changed. I wondered if he just didn't like pregnant women.

More than anything, I dreaded going to jail for the DUI. It was so hard to leave my baby. At only two weeks old, Alex and I needed to bond. I was leaving this newborn and my five-year-old daughter with Frank.

During my incarceration, Frank would drop Alex off at my grandmother's while he worked. When I could, I called collect to my grandmother's house so I could talk to Frank and check on the kids. I'd find out that Frank hadn't picked the kids up and hadn't called her. I'd try calling our house and he wouldn't answer. Now I was convinced he was cheating on me. Coincidentally, it was the same thing he was always accusing me of doing. I felt helpless and totally frustrated. I missed the kids terribly. I wanted to die. I lived for the visits when Frank would bring Alex to me. My baby slept on my chest and I never wanted to let go.

Six

SIN CITY

Childbirth and jail time behind us, Frank decided to take me to Vegas for a vacation. Once we checked into the room, we showered to go out for dinner and gambling. He made comments about the way other men were looking at me and got angry any time I spoke to another man. I had to sit with my hands clasped in front of me on the table at all times or he would think I was flirting.

    The next morning after breakfast, we walked around for awhile and did some sight-seeing. At night, we went out again for dinner and drinks. We had fun for a while. At about eleven, he said he wanted to go to the room. I wanted to stay and gamble. He got upset and ordered me to the room. We went up and I was mad to give up some much-needed fun. I really wanted to go back downstairs. I complained and told him I was leaving. Suddenly incensed, Frank grabbed me by the hair. He threw me in the room, locked the door, and shoved me against the wall. He grabbed my hair again and yanked my head into the table. I was too terrified to fight back. This was new and horrifying. He went ballistic for an hour, punching and kicking. In shock, I lay on the bed gasping until he stopped.

    Afterwards, I didn't know if I should call the police. Frank was pacing the room. I went for the phone and he ripped it out of the wall. I gave up trying before it got worse. I was sure he'd attack me again. He fell asleep by the door, guarding it with the ruined phone in his arms. We didn't have cell phones. I was trapped and mystified by this new Frank.

I tiptoed to the window to see how high up we were. We were three stories up. I checked the window latches and tried to decide whether I could jump. I knew if I did I'd probably break my legs or neck, so I turned to the bed and went to lie down. I couldn't sleep. The pain in my head and cut, swollen lip kept me awake. My mind couldn't let go of the violence.

The next morning, he acted like nothing ever happened. He had absolutely no explanation for the injuries on my face. It was as if he didn't see them. I told him I wanted to go home to Phoenix. He patronized me and said we should stay and have fun in Vegas. I still wanted to go home and insisted I was ready to leave, saying I needed to see my kids. At last we got our stuff together and left. I couldn't stop thinking about whether to call the police and how I would do it. But I knew if I did call the police, they wouldn't do anything because it had happened the night before.

On the drive home, Frank totally denied that he caused my hurt lip. He maintained that he didn't remember us having a fight. Real or faked, he had a total loss of memory. It made him livid that I would accuse him of hitting me. Driving around Hoover Dam, Frank assumed, "Oh, you're going to leave me?" He floored the accelerator around the dam like he wanted to kill us both. I was screaming, just begging him not to do it. We flew past cars, narrowly missing a few. I said I would stay with him. He calmed down. I didn't say anything else about my lip or head the whole way home.

Back in Phoenix, I considered calling the police, but I knew the Phoenix police wouldn't do anything about an incident that happened in Las Vegas. I put on heavy makeup and dark lipstick and went to get the kids.

After the Vegas trip, I lost the baby weight and noticed my husband was staying home more. I worked out to get back in shape and my husband was getting more jealous. He became hostile and thought he was entitled to know my every movement. He started accusing me of things and didn't want me going out.

After a few months, we decided to work our relationship out and to take another little trip by ourselves to get a short break from the kids. Frank wanted to go to Rocky Point, Mexico, just the two of us.

After driving several hours, we got there and found a hotel with available rooms. We went out to dinner, and again, the first couple nights were alright. Late into the third night, we drove Frank's truck to the beach. The truck got stuck in the sand and Frank was infuriated. He raged, getting really crazy and blaming me, pulling my hair and punching me. I cried, "Stop! Stop! Frank, you're hurting me!" But he wouldn't hear me. He pulled me out of the truck and threw me on the sand. He straddled my hips like he was going to rape me. I couldn't believe no one heard my cries. He pulled my skirt up and started fighting with me. I knew he was losing his mind so I decided not to fight back and to help him calm down. It seemed my only chance. Finally he stopped the beating, but he called me names over and over. I went back in the cab of the truck and he got into the bed of the pickup. I could feel my face was swollen and my head hurt. I was scared. I didn't know what he was going to do next. He was smoking in the truck bed and I was smoking in the front seat trying to calm my frayed nerves. Frank passed out from drinking. I didn't know what to do. The truck was still stuck in the sand. We were stuck on a beach in the middle of Mexico. All I could see was black sky for miles. I thought about walking, but we were so far from anything but beach.

I decided if I walked I could be found by the wrong kind of guys, which might be worse. So I decided to stay with the truck. When the sun came up, some Mexicans drove by in a truck. They asked if we needed help. I couldn't speak Spanish so Frank, who is fluent, talked to them. I wanted to tell them what happened to me, in hopes they would help, but I couldn't speak their language. The Mexicans helped us pull the truck out of the sand. Then we drove back to our hotel. Frank was acting like nothing happened. When we got into the room, I grabbed my things and took off for the door. He chased me and I ran to the reception desk and tried frantically to explain what was going on. They saw Frank running after me. When my husband saw me in the reception area, he calmly went back to our room. I sat and drank water for a while. I didn't know what to do next. I talked to the desk clerks who were checking guests into their rooms and asked where the police station was or what I should do. They pointed out where the police were, so I walked to the station. They couldn't speak English either. I was trying to tell them my husband beat me and I needed to get back to Phoenix. All they said was, "No se," shaking their heads; they didn't understand me.

I sat on a bench outside and smoked, contemplating what to do. Somebody walked by who spoke broken English. I told them, "Mi esposo," and demonstrated him hitting me. He pointed to the bus station, which was quite a walk. It was a depressed, slum-like area. I walked there, watching my back. I was scared of nationals and scared of Frank. Men were honking and making gestures at me. I found the station and tried to explain that I needed to get to Phoenix. Only a couple people spoke a little English. They gave me the bus schedule. But I didn't understand the Spanish. Defeated, I finally gave up and headed back to the hotel. What if I got on a bus and ended up in the wrong place. South America, maybe?

Frank drove by and told me to get in the truck. I did. We went to the hotel and gathered our things. I tried to keep things peaceful.

Chapter Six | Sin City

He was really trying to be apologetic but there was no sincerity in his voice or face.

We drove four hours back to Phoenix. He kept asking if I needed anything to eat or drink. I didn't speak. I was thinking of how to deal with all this. When we got to Phoenix, we went straight to my grandmother's. I didn't want to tell them about it, especially with the kids there. I covered the bruises with heavy foundation and no one asked any questions.

It was around Halloween and Alex was 10 months old. We had a nice house then, and we were fighting a lot. He would ask what I was doing all day and talk and complain about the way I was dressed and how I took care of Alex. He wanted to know everything and would ask me detailed questions about the whole day, but I wouldn't dare ask him about himself. He wouldn't tell me anything about what he was doing or where he was when I called. Still, I had to answer to him about everything. One night we were arguing and the kids were asleep. He got mad because I would not have sex with him. He pushed me off the bed and then I got mad and started cursing. I went into the living room to sleep. I cried all night. He came out and was mad because I wouldn't go back to bed with him. He made me get up and talk to him. He got mean and yelled, calling me names. I tried to get up and go to my room. He pinned me down. He always did things like that when the kids were asleep or gone. He started to slap me. I tried to fight back. Frank stood up and pulled a big knife out of his pants. He stuck it to my face and said, "Don't move!" and started to wave it around my face and body, playing head games with me and trying to scare me. He liked having that control. He moved away and disappeared for a minute, possibly into the bathroom, then came back and told me to go to bed.

I lay in bed watching the sun come up. I noticed slash marks on his back. He'd reached behind and slashed himself with the knife so that if I'd called the police to report our fight, he could tell them I'd cut him and *I* would've gone to jail. He always thought faster than me. I'm glad I didn't call the cops that night. But the next day we woke up fighting again. He didn't go to work and I would not talk to him. I was kind of in shock about the whole knife thing. I believed deep inside he wasn't going to use it. It was about power and control. When he had the knife in his hand, he would walk around like a sergeant. He would put his leg on the couch where I was sitting, elbow on his knee, and swat the knife around to make sure I saw it.

When I looked into his eyes, I didn't see Frank—he was another person. We fought all the rest of the day because I wouldn't talk to him. Chelsea was in school and Alex was playing around the house. Frank started getting crazy again. He yelled and acted like he was going to hit me. He was getting violent. I was not going to go through this again, but I was still scared from the previous night. When he wasn't around, I called the cops. When they arrived, I ran outside crying and told them my husband was violent, getting ready to hit me, and I was scared. I told them he'd pulled a knife last night.

Frank walked out of the house totally calm and said, "Calm down, Tracy. She's going crazy. Now, now, Tracy calm down. Everything is all right." He said, "Officer she gets like this sometimes." I told them he'd put a knife to my face last night. They asked if I had any marks. I said no, and Frank said, "I do" and lifted his shirt.

The cops said, "You should have called last night when she did that. There's nothing we can do now." Frank told them, "I understand. I wouldn't want my wife to go to jail anyway." He made me look crazy in front of the cops. Like I was a nutcase exaggerating. They were laughing because I was crying and Frank was so calm. They believed him, told us to quit fighting, and they left.

I was shocked that I had no one to help me now. No family,

no cops. I started to really get scared. *What if no one ever believes me?* We went inside. He told me if I ever did that again, he'd find a way to put me in jail. For a few days, I was in another world—I couldn't believe this was happening. My marriage, my life, the police, everything! Every night when I went to sleep, I would see those three long slash marks on his back when he was sleeping and think, *"Why is this happening to me? It's so weird. He's my husband and he's supposed to love me."* I just couldn't figure the whole thing out. We went on about our lives and I tried to get over it. He wouldn't talk about it. It was like he didn't know, or didn't remember, what he'd done.

Life with Frank was unpredictable. If things were good, we'd spend our time talking about the kids and work. We'd have barbecues, and go through all the motions of a "normal" couple. Around friends and family, Frank was on his best behavior. An outsider would have never believed what was brewing underneath. I lived for the days that were good and dreaded the days that weren't. The anticipation of the ever-ready flare-up kept me in a constant state of confusion and insecurity.

One day, as I was leaving the house to see friends, he decided he didn't like the way I was dressed. He snapped, "Where do you think you're going dressed like that?" Without waiting for me to answer, "You're not going anywhere dressed like that and you need to go change." I spat back, "No! You're not my dad, you're my husband." Frank pushed me towards our bedroom and barked, "Go change!" He pushed me so hard I fell. I had high-heeled sandals on and my whole body weight fell on my left foot. I couldn't get up and still he said, "Get up and go change!" The pain shot up my leg; "I *can't* get up!" He said, "You're a liar. Get up." "Frank, my foot hurts I think it's broken and I need to go the hospital." "I'm not taking you to the hospital." "I need to call my mom then," I said, wincing with pain.

Frank pulled me up. He was trying to make me walk. I just couldn't do it, so he finally agreed, "OK, we'll go the hospital."

In the emergency department, they put me and my husband in an exam room. The doctors came in and asked what had happened. I couldn't possibly tell them the truth because Frank was right there with me and if I told the doctor what had happened, my husband would have gotten really mad. Frank was playing the part of the concerned husband and their suspicions were never aroused. It never occurred to the doctors to separate us to give me the chance to speak freely. So, I told them I fell down the stairs. Simple fix for my broken foot, they put me in a cast. Not so simple emotionally.

I was seriously thinking I'd better leave my husband. He'd gotten more abusive. Who knows what he'll break next time? Abuse always escalates. I knew that from my mother's husbands and boyfriends. All sorts of thoughts ran through my head; now I was in a cast and I had nowhere to go. I had a baby by him. My mom lived with my grandmother and I was on crutches and I still couldn't work. So I had to stay with him.

At home, Frank would help me up and down the stairs. He never apologized. He denied it ever happened. I couldn't do anything. I had my mom take a picture of my leg just to have. It may come in useful someday. I knew deep down inside I needed to leave him. But I couldn't until my leg healed. I had a cast on for the next eight weeks.

The doctors who treated me told me I would have problems for the rest of my life due to damaged metacarpals. I got my cast off and I started to plan how to leave Frank. One day I said I was going to move in with my friend and he went crazy. We were upstairs in our room. I was sitting on a chair in front of my makeup table. He grabbed me by the hair and shouted, "If you leave me I will kill you!" He threw me on the floor and sat on my stomach, choking me. I tried to scream but had no voice with his hands squeezing down on my throat. I was thrashing from side to side, trying to throw him off balance. *God,* I thought, *please don't let this be happening again, please!* Frank pushed his thumb in my left eye really hard, gouging so that my vision went black on that side. I thought I would lose my eye. I got a hold of the phone and called 9-1-1 and, gasping, told them what was happening.

Soon there were helicopters circling overhead. Frank left the house and took off running. I showed the cops my eye and told them about the fight. It was my first actual police report, more than just a call to the police to come to the house and stop a fight, and I was going to make sure it stuck. They looked for Frank but never found him.

Hours later he came back home and he knew for sure I was going to leave him this time. The next day he went to the courthouse and got an Order of Protection against me so I would look like the bad guy. He was getting smart now and trying to discredit me. He was setting me up.

In a couple days, he made the most of his opportunity. I got home from work and he called the police, telling them I was near him and in violation of the Order. They told me I could not be near the house and I needed to get out of the area. So angry at the outright lie, I attempted to explain to them it was my house, and in my name. They said, "It doesn't matter." I had twenty minutes to get all my stuff out. Disgusted, I called my friend Martina. We had twenty minutes and a lot to do. So we stuffed as much of my belongings as we could in the back of her truck, including the washer and dryer, clothes—as much as we could get our hands on. It looked like one of those grand prize shopping sprees where they give you a cart and let you shove everything off the shelves into it, as you make a mad dash up and down the aisles.

The police watched it. Ultimately, it was a good thing because I wanted to leave him anyway; this gave me a safe way to do it.

Frank was sitting near the police laughing and smirking thinking it was a big joke. He'd succeeded in publicly making me look stupid.

Chelsea and I moved out, but Frank kept Alex. We stayed at my friend's house in a spare room and put all my stuff in a garage to store. My husband still had a lot of our things. I would drive by my house, and if he wasn't there I could sneak in to get more of my belongings. Most of all, I wanted to get my son. On one trip, when I drove over there, the place looked empty so I went in and it was all dirty. Used dishes were left crusting in the sink. He'd left clothes on the floor. It was dusty and had crumbs on the carpet. One thing I'd always had was pride in my homes. I was a cleaner by nature and kept the house neat, fresh, and welcoming. This was an insult.

The house was rented in my name so I knew I needed to clean it. The last thing I needed was to be held accountable for a mess he'd made when I wasn't even living there. I'd had my credit ruined by a past boyfriend and wasn't about to let it happen again.

I called Frank's mom in Texas and I found out he was there with my son. He'd been there for days. Frustrated, there was nothing I could do about it at this point until I got my life together. Frank knew exactly what would hurt me the most—taking Alex.

My mother came over to help me clean. Without Frank there, I could claim my house back. While we were cleaning, some neighbors came over and they said they'd seen Frank leaving. It was good to see my old neighbors again, just to sit around and shoot the breeze.

Their friend, Cory, was with them. We were introduced and I told him I was renting a U-Haul and moving soon. Cory offered to help. Glad for the help, we exchanged phone numbers. He helped me and my mother clean that night and we kept in touch. About two weeks later, I found a place to live so I called Cory and said, "If the offer's still good, I'm ready for the help."

Chapter Six | Sin City

Cory rented the U-Haul for me. He helped me move the rest of my stuff, put all my beds together, and connected appliances. My new home was a great little two-story townhouse on the outside corner of two quiet streets. Our complex had a community pool and faced the garages of the neighboring town houses. My Arcadia doors faced the most quiet of the two streets on which sat a school for children with disabilities. The inside of the house was clean, with beautiful vaulted ceilings. I loved it and was anxious to start a new life without threats, false accusations, and constantly feeling that the slightest provocation would set Frank off. At the same time I felt conflicted. Marriage, I believed, was for life. I couldn't wrap my mental arms around the idea of ending mine.

After my foot healed, I started dancing again at the same club where I'd worked on and off for years, and I got a second job as a medical assistant. I worked days at an outpatient clinic and nights at the club. Cory and I became very good friends, and he got along with my mother, who was now living with me. He would help me with everything. I finally started to get my life together. I was ready to get my son back. Cory said he would go to Texas and get him. Tempting thought, but I said, "No, we need to do this the right way." I began to call lawyers and to meet with some of them. They all told me the same thing, that Frank was my husband and he was allowed to have our son in another state, whether I'd consented or not. It would cost me several hundred an hour to try to get Alex back. I didn't have that kind of money. There was nothing I could do, so I tried to live my life the best that I could, but I ached for Alex every minute. Frank had to have known that would happen to me. Frank had to have known I would desperately miss Alex and not be able to afford lawyers to try to get him back. This world is made for people who have money, like Frank, and they knew how the game was played.

After being in Texas about a month, my husband started calling my grandmother's house, trying to find out where I was and asking her for my phone number. I had already asked my grandmother not to ever tell him where I was and so she told him she didn't know.

He called her every day looking for me. Eventually, my grandmother told me she was getting sick of him calling her. Though she was always supportive of me, Frank was disrupting her life. I told her to go ahead and give him my number but not my address.

Frank called me to tell me how much he loved me and missed me. The words had no meaning anymore. There was a time it would have meant everything to me to hear, "I love you." Now, I didn't believe it and I didn't trust it.

I asked if I could talk to Alex and he wouldn't let me, but he begged and begged to come back and live with me. I refused because of the abuse. He was relentless; every day he would call me and I would call back to try to ask the family if I could talk to Alex. No one would let me; they kept saying he was in the bathroom or out playing. Two-year-old Alex was being used as the dangling carrot—always beyond my reach.

Worn down, I sat one day with my mom and talked about everything with her and my nine-year-old daughter. Everyone in my family said, "Just let him come back. We all miss Alex so much." The next day when Frank called me, he said his former boss in Phoenix was going to give him his job back. If Frank could just live with me, until he got re-established, he'd bring Alex back. If things didn't work out in our marriage, he convinced me, he'd move out and we'd share custody.

I needed to have my son back and gave in to his promise. I believed it was worth a try if Alex could come home. Frank promised to start driving back to Phoenix first thing in the morning and be here in two days. True to his word, when he got to Phoenix, he called me and told me he was at a motel room and had my son with him. He wanted me to meet him at the motel so I could show him where I lived.

Chapter Six | Sin City

After four long and painful months, I finally held my son! He was so big and cute. I'd missed him so much and couldn't stop hugging him! He still loved me every bit as much as the day he was taken.

Back at my new house, my mom and Chelsea ran to the door and hugged Alex. It was a good day and we were all very happy and relieved. They got settled in, but I was a little scared I was making a big mistake. My husband was being very nice and he said he really wanted to try. It was early July and definitely pool weather in Arizona. "Do you guys want to see the community pool?" I offered.

While we were getting ready to go swimming, Cory called and asked what we were doing. I told him I was going to go swimming with my husband and kids. He started to cry and said, "I hope he doesn't hurt you again. I hope he's good to you." This I didn't need; an emotional male friend and a suspicious husband. I hung up on Cory. I couldn't talk to him with Frank there.

I was very independent now and my husband could see that. Before he left, I was entirely wrapped around his finger, but not anymore. I'd found my own way of life again. I began a doll collection and for the first time I found something that I enjoyed, just for me. Most of all, I had found *myself* without him around. Time and distance can do a lot. So things between us just weren't the same. When we went to bed at night and he would try to lie next to me, I really didn't want him near me. The physical attraction was gone, the emotional attraction was dead. He knew that I was independent now and the love I had for him had faded away.

My Mom and Dad with me in 1970.

A photo of me from the Arizona State Roller Skating Championships.

My brother and me.

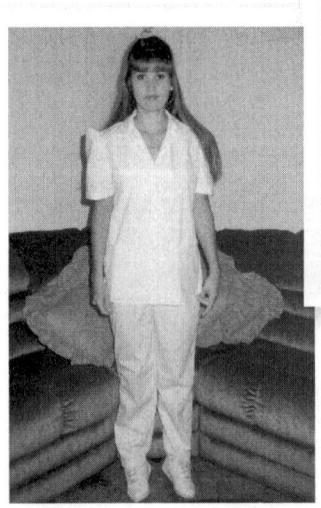

Me before going to work as a nurse's assistant.

My friend and me (left) with Jinx, the truck driver.

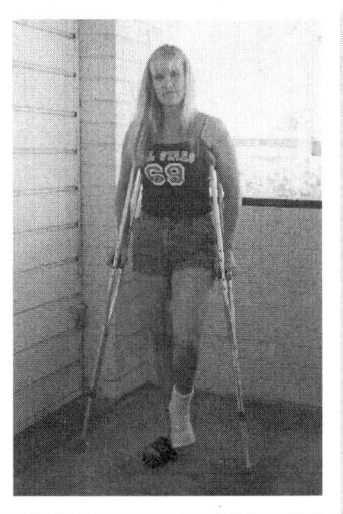

My broken foot from when Frank pushed me down.

One of the events where I spoke about domestic violence and told my story.

My son standing outside his bedroom at the top of the stairs.

A photo of me, after the scars on my face healed.

Seven

DEAD WOMAN WALKING

As hard as I tried, I didn't feel the same about Frank, but I was glad to be with my son. My husband was trying to be a good husband and good father, but I just didn't have the same feelings anymore. You can't go through that much pain and rejection without feeling resentful and hurt. I wasn't wrapped around his finger anymore and I had gotten over him. Independence felt too good. Life being just Tracy suited me. I had been beaten down time and again. My self-esteem had wasted away. Now, bit by bit during my time alone, I felt buoyed up, and I wasn't about to let it go.

Sleeping side-by-side felt wrong and uncomfortable. It wasn't natural to have Frank in the same bed, or even in the same house. I was very distant and knew deep inside things weren't going to work between us. He had done so many bad things to me. I just needed time away from him and now I'd had four months apart. It helped me get over him.

On August 1, 2001, I went to work at the clinic in the morning. Having gotten his old job back, Frank was off to a construction site. While I was at work, my mom watched Alex. My daughter was at her friend's house after sleeping over the night before.

Frank called me at the clinic and said he'd gotten off work early and was at home. Just then, my friend Cory arrived at the house to borrow twenty dollars from my mother. My husband asked him who he was. Cory told Frank his name and said he had helped me and my mother move. When my husband called me, he demanded, "Is this who you've been sleeping with the whole time we were separated?" I said, "No, he helped me put things together and helped Mom and me move." I told him to leave me alone and that I was working. He kept yelling, so I got off the phone; to Cory he said, "Let's go talk" and they went for a ride in Frank's truck. Frank bought him a pack of cigarettes, a hot dog, and a Coke. He was trying to charm him, show him the nice-guy routine. Cory was always broke, and it didn't take much to talk him into free food and cigarettes. He wasn't scared of anything and easily went along for the ride.

They drove to the park and my husband kept demanding to know if he had had sex with me. Cory insisted, "No, I love your wife and mother-in-law to death, but I just helped them move and we're just all really good friends." "I would understand," Frank said, "if you had sex with my wife, because she's very beautiful."

Cory insisted again we hadn't had sex. Frank went home and Cory left in his Jeep. My husband kept calling me at work and I told him to leave me alone. If this kept up I'd lose my job. I hung up, but minutes later he showed up at the clinic. I went out to the lobby to talk with him where he was frantically asking me again and again if I'd had sex with Cory and if I wanted to be with him. I tried to calm him down, worried that I would be fired for him making a scene, and I asked him to leave. I said we'd talk about this when I get home. He finally left. My coworkers heard bits and pieces of the argument. Thankfully, no patients were in the lobby. I had about two hours left before the end of my shift. I dreaded going home and facing the inevitable fight with him.

At four o'clock, I left my day job at the clinic. I was going to have to get ready for my night job. I stopped at the mailbox and saw my neighbor in his driveway. I asked him if he wanted to go to happy hour because I was fighting with my husband and was going to need a drink. "I have to go into the house and fight with him now," I said. "I'm going to be stressed out later."

I went into the house with my mail and when I got inside; predictably, my husband started arguing with me. He followed me into my bedroom and kept asking me if I had sex with Cory. I was tired of it, we'd been over this, and I didn't want to argue with him. I took off my shoes to shower before my second job. I glared at my husband and said, "Look, Cory is my friend, that's **all** he is, so leave me alone!" Relentless, he kept arguing with me. "Look", I told him, "I don't want Cory and I don't want you. I don't want *anyone*. Do you understand?"

Enraged, Frank threw me on the bed and called me a fucking bitch. Leaning over, he started choking me. I was trying to fight him off and I tried screaming for him to leave me alone. Hearing our shouts, my mom came down the stairs. Frank got off me. My mom said, "What's going on?" I said, "He just choked me and I'm leaving for a while." He was blocking the entry to the front door so I couldn't get past. "I need to leave for a while!" and he hissed, "You're not going anywhere!" Mom said, "Let her leave if she wants to leave for a little while." He grabbed her by the hair then reached out and grabbed me too, latching onto my French braid. Spitting fury, he seethed, "I'm going to kill the both of you!"

He pulled us both by our hair into the kitchen. It made us stumble, and in a heap, we were all on the floor. My mother and I were scrambling to get our footing. Frank grabbed for the knife drawer. The whole drawer fell out and silverware scattered all over the floor.

Frank grabbed an eight-inch, serrated knife. He started to go crazy with it. Flashing it back and forth. Slashing towards us up into the air and back down. Lightning speed. Mom was in front of Frank and I was still held behind him. I was unspeakably terrified.

All I could see was blood, specks of blood, little bits. It splattered the walls and pooled on the floor.

I didn't know if it was coming from Mom or me. I glanced up and saw the kitchen lights as the fight was going on. I saw spots before my eyes. I looked to my left, saw my son sitting on the stairs screaming and crying. I begged, "Stop, Frank—please stop!" I told him Alex was crying. That didn't faze him. I cried, "Everybody calm down!" but that didn't help either.

We were all in our tiny kitchen. He was going up and down with the knife, cutting everywhere on my arms and hands, while he held my mom with his left hand. He stood in front of us both, striking at her, striking at me. He let go of my mom and pulled me by the hair to my bedroom. Now in the bedroom, he started punching me, still with the knife in his hand. Hoping for escape, I quickly looked over outside my bedroom's French doors, which led into the living room. My mom had crawled from the kitchen to the living room to see what was happening to me. I could see her, but I still didn't know where Alex was, I could only hear him screaming.

My mother sat up on her knees with her hands out in the air, her bloody palms facing the ceiling. We looked at each other; then Frank began stabbing me in the face. He was taking advantage of my attention turned to her.

As I looked at her, she said, "I'm bleeding." Her voice was soft, sad, and scared. Blood was coming out of her neck above her collar bone, dripping down her chest. She was looking over at me as I was being stabbed. I saw panic in her expression. She looked dazed and surprised. I couldn't help her, and she couldn't help me. She looked so sad. We were only ten feet from each other and it seemed like miles.

Frank dragged me around to the side of my bed. My view was blocked by a wall, so I couldn't see her anymore. He punched me and threw me back down. His shoed foot kicked me repeatedly in my ribs. I started fighting back. With everything I had, I kicked his groin, and he flew back against the dresser. I tried to escape through the Arcadia door to my patio. Now he was outraged. His face contorted with anger and his eyes became glazed.

I didn't know where my mother was. I figured she had called the cops and help was coming soon. I prayed that the police were on their way.

I knew it wasn't safe to try to get out. When his anger escalated, he punched my jaw with full force and I slammed back across the bed. My head was throbbing. He grabbed me off the bed by my French braid. Now I was on the floor alongside my bed in a narrow space beside the wall. He held the braid tight and sawed it off with the knife. Hair was everywhere, knotted with blood. He said, "Nobody will ever want you again!" He blasted a kick in my groin, pain shot up my back. "Now you can't have sex anymore. You'll never have sex as long as you live!"

He tried to cut my throat with the knife. I held my hands up in front of me, protecting my face, and they caught the jabs of the blade. I buried my face into the carpet to try to keep him from getting my jugular. He sliced me from the middle of the back of my neck all the way around to the right towards my throat. My body was on fire in agonizing pain. I was eating the carpet trying to keep him from getting to my throat.

I saw blood everywhere. When he punched me, blood would spray all over the walls. I could see my hair all over the floor; part of it was in one big chunk, knotted and full of blood. That was the better part of my braid.

He roared, "No one will ever want you as long as you live!" Uhhh! I gasped as he pulled me up by my shorn hair and punched me in the face, then threw me back to the floor. I blacked out for a couple seconds.

I could barely fight back. It felt like my ribs were cracked. My chest burned and I had lost so much blood. I was weak and if I fought back, it just got worse, and he got angrier. It was almost not worth fighting him.

He grabbed me by my hair again and pulled me to my feet. I think he wanted to move me. He made me walk with him while he held my hair with the knife in his hand. He pulled me out of my bedroom and through the living room. If I hadn't tried to walk, he would've been dragging me. I looked for my mother but didn't see her anywhere. Frank pulled me by my hair, dragging me toward the steps. When we turned the corner by the front entry, I tried to run for the door. I tried to get out, but he grabbed me by my hair and got really mad. He yanked my hair harder and forced me up the stairs. Once on the second floor, I passed my children's rooms. I glanced towards Alex's room and saw him in there. Frank told him to stay in his room. Then, as Frank took me in my mom's room, he snarled, "I told you 'till death do us part'," then he pinned me to the floor and started to cut me again. With searing pain, I felt him slice my nose. Out of the corner of my eye, I could see my nose was dangling back and forth on the right side of my face. Lashing out, he cut me by my right ear. My ears filled with so much blood, I could barely hear. I felt like I was underwater, hearing Frank's voice bubbling above me. Vomit whooshed up my throat and spilled out to the floor beside me. He continued to stab me. When he stabbed my left shoulder, the force of his anger broke the knife's handle from the blade. The blade fell to the floor.

When the knife broke, he blamed me. Look what I've done! He blamed me about his family and said, "It's all your fault, look what you made me do now! My family was so proud of me because I was trying to be a good dad. My dad was so proud of me for the first time in my life! Now look what I've done." He started to bring up his whole childhood. He was ranting and pacing around the house.

I found out later he called my grandmother and told her to call his mother in Texas. We didn't have long distance service and he wanted her to call him at my house. A year later, Frank testified at the criminal trial that he told his mother, "Mom, Tracy got cut ..." He spoke to his mom on the phone for a long time, probably ten minutes. I found out later that his mother called my grandmother and told her Frank called about me "getting cut." My grandmother called 9-1-1.

Now Frank could hear the cops outside. The SWAT team was on the roof. He was getting scared. He left me momentarily and went downstairs. I could hear the blinds moving and drawers opening and closing. I was visualizing in my mind what he was doing. What was he getting? What was he hiding?

Still lying on the floor, I could hardly move, my body shrieked with pain. I could hear Frank in the kitchen. If I could pull myself up to move, it would be my chance to get out. I wanted to jump from my mother's window, but I couldn't get to it. My brain wanted to, but my body wouldn't obey. The phone kept ringing. While Frank was downstairs, my son came to me. I was lying on the floor between my mother's bed and the wall. Both thumbs were hanging off from the defensive wounds and my nose was swinging on the side of my face. Alex looked down at me and lifted his little shirt up. He showed me his two squirt guns and said, "Do you want me to shoot Dada?" I had little energy to speak. I whispered, "Just go to your room, *please*. Go to your room."

Frank came back in my mom's room and began ranting again, but, thankfully, the knife was broken.

I heard the phone ring again. He picked up the cordless phone and was pacing around the room. I could tell by his side of the conversation that he was talking to his mother. I heard him say, "I stabbed Tracy. Mama, I'm going to prison for the rest of my life. I'm just going to let this cop shoot me when they get here."

The police were everywhere outside. I could hear them yelling and cars driving up. I heard stomping on the roof. Frank kept looking nervously out the bedroom window and standing on my mother's toilet looking out the bathroom window.

He had been torturing me for a couple hours but it seemed much, much more. Time passed painfully slowly. I worried for my children. Maybe, as his natural son, Alex would be safe. Chelsea was due home from her sleepover and I didn't doubt for a second Frank could kill her. By now, I prayed, my mother was somewhere safe.

The police and negotiators kept calling the house. I could hear Frank saying, "I will shoot a cop. I have a .38 and I'm gonna shoot a cop." He leaned over to me and put the phone by my mouth. I couldn't talk. I wanted to scream. I couldn't with him standing right there. When they asked if I was OK, I wanted to tell them I'd been stabbed a bunch of times and was dying. I just moaned. Did they honestly think I could answer that question with him breathing fire in my face? Would I risk myself more to say anything, knowing it would ignite him? That phone should've been my life line but using it would kill me. He took the phone away. The negotiators called again. They wanted him to come out, but he asked to talk to his brother in Texas. They called Texas and had his brother call Frank. "Geez," I thought sarcastically, "why not ask for a Big Mac while you're at it?"

I wondered how long I could hang on. I was barely breathing, which was a blessing of sorts because my ribs shuttered with every breath.

I believed I could die if I wanted to just let go. All I had to do was close my eyes and go to sleep. I kept telling myself, *Stay alive, stay alive. The kids have no place to go if I die.* I still didn't know where my mom was. I could tell Frank was getting agitated again. I saw him pick up big silver sewing scissors from my mother's sewing kit. I thought, *Oh my God! He's going to use these on me now! I'm going to have to play dead before he uses these.*

I tried to play dead and he would kick me. Testing me to see if I was alive. I tried not to breathe and he'd kick me again. He spat, "You're still not dead? Why won't you die, bitch?" All I could think was, *How come the cops won't come in and save me? Alright.* I convinced myself, *the only chance I have to live is to play dead the best I can so he won't hurt me anymore.* I was sure this time he'd be put away for good. That faith was keeping me alive. I needed to live for my children.

He would kick or punch me really hard and I moved involuntarily. He knew I wasn't really dead. He began to calm down again and I thought the only thing left is to talk to him. I said, "All I needed was time, baby. That's all, that's all. I love you." "Why didn't you tell me that before?" He cried, "Why didn't you tell me you needed time?"

"You didn't give me a chance."

"Now look what I've done."

I told him to run. Get out the back window and run. I was trying everything and he was calming down. Frank lit a cigarette. He went to the bathroom and returned with a wet washcloth. He started to clean my face and body. He offered me a drag off the cigarette. He leaned over and put the cigarette in my mouth and wiped my face with the cloth. Then he gave me his wedding ring and went in Alex's room. He was talking to Alex. I couldn't tell what he was saying though. I heard him go downstairs and pace around. He opened the door slowly to take a peek outside. I heard loud noises and the door flew open and thudded against the wall. I heard Frank get tackled.

There were thumping footsteps as several people ran up the stairs. I could hear things bang against the walls. They all ran over to me in masks and, calling to the others, yelled, "There's a live one up here!"

Phoenix Police Department Supplemental Report
Reporting Officer: Frank Spitler
Narrative (*excerpt*)

> 1825 Hours. Officer One found the victim, Tracy Stombres, lying on the floor at the foot of the bed in the upstairs south bedroom. Officer Kilgore also made entry into that bedroom at the same time. Tracy Stombres was lying on her left side, with her head facing south. I could see a lot of blood on her person, and on the carpet where she was lying. Then asked for the fire department paramedics. While waiting for the paramedics I spoke to Tracy to access her condition. She was alert and was in a lot of pain. I asked her about her injuries. She told me that her husband stabbed had her with a knife in her neck, throat, hands, and face. She stated that she was also kicked in the lower portion of her body. Officer Underwood treated Tracy for some of her injuries, and also stood by until the paramedics took over treating her.

> 1829 Hours. The paramedics began to treat Tracy. While the paramedics were treating Tracy, she stated that Frank, her husband had stabbed her mother in the living room and she was stabbed in the kitchen. Officer Underwood was also present at this time, when she made these statements. Tracy also stated that she had been laying there for hours, and was unable to move.

A man's soft voice said, "Are you OK?" It was over! All I could do was cry. *I'm finally saved!* The officer asked me questions like, "Who did this to you?" I could barely croak out the words, "My husband." All I could think was I was alive and going to live! I'd begun to think no one would ever help me. Minutes later, a paramedic kneeled next to me. He cut my bra and clothes off to check my wounds. More paramedics came in. There were firefighters and a SWAT team. They put me in a blue body sling with handles and carried me down the stairs. They laid me on a rolling gurney. I could see so many vehicles, TV news trucks, and people all over, up and down the block. I held my bleeding hands in the air. I didn't want to touch anything, it would hurt too much. They rolled me down the street. I could see yellow caution tape everywhere. I was rolled past curious eyes and speculating voices. My whole block was there. I felt like I was on exhibit. All I could think of was, *where's my mom? Where's my mom?*

They put me into the ambulance. They cleaned me up fast and inserted an I.V. I asked where my mother was. They said they thought she was taken to the hospital. I asked if she was at the same one I was going to and they said they thought she'd gone to another one.

Paramedics were naming my stab wounds to each other. "Right elbow superficial." "Left shoulder deep." "Right thigh deep." They called ahead to the hospital and told them we were coming. We re-routed half-way there; the hospital where were going was closed for construction so we had to go to another. Kind hands worked on me as I listened to the sirens. We went so fast. I was nauseated again. We pulled up to the emergency department. I recognized a nurse I knew—an ex-dancer. In her eyes I saw shock and concern. Then I blacked out.

Eight

DEADLY AWAKENING

I woke up hours later, after emergency surgery performed by the Chief of Plastic Surgery, Dr. Mosharrafa. I would later call my "my miracle worker." It took four pints of blood to replenish my blood loss.

I was wheeled down the hallway where my grandparents and children were waiting. My grandmother and daughter came to my side and comforted me with words of love and assurance. I had stitches and staples all over me, a regular Raggedy Ann. My hands were swaddled in lengths of gauze and resembled boxing gloves. My fingertips barely stuck out.

I was rolled into ICU, where only my grandmother was allowed. For my safety, she devised a code word that a selected few would know. Only those with the password could see me. She chose "Hugs" from the stuffed bears the firefighters had given my children at the scene because the bears had the word "Hugs" on them.

Until we need them ourselves, we often take for granted toy drives held by firefighters and law enforcement. They take on new meaning when your own child is offered comfort after trauma.

I was on a lot of painkillers and anxiety pills. I was really freaked out. Any little noise would make me jump. I asked my grandmother where my mother was. But she was very vague. I was so out of it, I didn't think much of it. I thought, oddly, maybe my mother was mad at me.

My grandparents and kids left late into the night, and at about one in the morning, the detectives came in. They asked me to tell them the whole story. As I told them, they were getting sarcastic with me, saying they'd heard a different version from Frank. Honestly, when *don't* they hear a different version? They told me he was charged with aggravated assault and had a bond for 80,000 dollars. Since you only have to come up with ten percent, it would be peanuts for his family to wire the money. I was stunned, "You mean he can be out tonight?" Sarcastically, "I'm going to sleep well. Are you guys crazy?" As if it was their doing. "He tried to kill me for hours and you guys are only charging him with aggravated assault and $8,000 will get him out! He'll be out tonight to finish me off! I had to play dead! I thought for sure he would be away for good this time. I can't believe this."

"We don't set the bonds, the Maricopa County District Attorney does. We didn't know how bad you were until now. But it's not up to us."

I was very argumentative with the detectives. Something about minimal charges and light bond infuriated me. The painkillers were making me feel groggy and sick. They looked at all my wounds. I showed the detectives how my hair had been cut off and more was falling out. There was still blood in my knotted hair. I'd been cleaned for surgery, but not bathed.

I asked the detectives where my mom was. They said they thought she was in another hospital. It was getting on my nerves that no one seemed to know. After the detectives left, they sent a female officer to take pictures of me. It would be a year before I would learn the impact of only having "after" shots when I was bandaged and stitched up.

Chapter Eight | Deadly Awakening

She took pictures of all my wounds and cuts. There were forty by her count. When she was done, I finally got to sleep. It would only be a few more hours before the sun was up.

Real sleep was impossible, but I drifted in and out. Drugs and medication competed against certain terror. I was so scared my husband would get out with a mere $8,000, quickly supplied, no doubt, by his family. He could always get his mom to put her house up for the money and I had no doubt she would. I'm sure that first night the nurses thought I was losing my mind. Every time they walked in the room, I would jump. A counselor had to come and talk with me. She gave me more pills, these for anxiety, depression, and sleep. I kept waking up anyway and having weird nightmares. The attack kept replaying over and over in my head. I couldn't sleep. I woke up to a nurse looking down at me the next morning. She said, "You are a very lucky girl." I grumbled, "Lucky, what do mean lucky? I'm hardly lucky." She said, "Yes, because you happened to come in the emergency room last night while the best surgeon in Arizona was in the trauma room. He said he wanted to take care of you and fix your face up, and he did. You are going to be just fine, I promise you."

A pastor, a counselor, and a couple nurses came in and arranged themselves by my bed. I watched them expectantly. They told me that my mom is in a "better place." She didn't make it.

"What do you mean she didn't make it?" Instant panic.

"Your mom passed away."

Mom?

I started crying.

I had so much guilt inside. I was grieving. I didn't want anyone around me.

They prayed with me anyway. I think more for themselves than for me. It seemed to make them feel better. I was staring numbly at the walls and into space. All I could think about was the attack replaying over and over again in my mind. That day I slept and took pills to sleep more. I thought about everything. I was so scared of everyone. I thought Frank would send someone to kill me. I had nightmares all night.

Cory came to see me later in the evening. Visiting hours were almost over. He told me that he had received a voice message from Frank saying, "how do you like your bitch now?"

When I woke up the next day, the nurse told me the news people wanted to come talk to me. She asked if I was up to it. Having been all over the news two nights before, the media wanted word from the survivor. I told her I'd do the interview. My friend came and helped me comb my hair. There was dried blood caked in it and it was completely knotted up. My hands and arms were bandaged up to my elbows. I couldn't take care of myself.

She brushed as gently as possible and handfuls of hair came out. We set the hair next to the bed. When we were done the news people came in. There were four of them. They asked me, "in your own words," what happened. I described in plain words that I had left my husband for a while and he'd come back. We got into a fight and he killed my mom, stabbed me forty times, kicked me in the groin, and told me I'd never have sex again. He was trying to kill me and asked me how come I won't die. I told them he could be out tonight, right now. Because his bond was only 80,000 dollars. All he needs is $8,000 to get out. I told the news people he only got charged with aggravated assault and second-degree murder. I told them this is why women stay with abusive men. Because it's safer that way. No one ever makes these men pay for what they do.

As they were leaving, one of the newswomen bent down and kissed me on my cheek. "I went through something like this a long time ago and you're going to be just fine." Tears welled in my eyes and I thanked her. After they left, the nurse came and told me more news people wanted to come in but she'd told them no.

Chapter Eight | Deadly Awakening

I needed to rest—it was enough for one day.

I was just lying there alone. I had so much going through my head. I had no mom, no husband, and I was going to be really ugly and scarred on my face, neck, arms, and hands. My hair was cut off. I was completely stunned. In many ways, this was predictable. Living with Frank had been beating after beating, always getting worse, which is always what happens. He had told me many times he would kill me. That's why I'd tried to end the marriage in the first place. But my mother? That changed everything.

A few hours later, a couple friends came to see me. They told me they saw me on the news a few times and had recorded some of the newscasts. The phone rang, and it was Detective D'Angelo. "I have good news," he said. "The District Attorney, Rick Romley, saw you on the news and raised the bond to $350,000. That means it would take a payment of $35,000 to get him out. And the charges were raised to attempted murder."

That was a small comfort. I was feeling a little better at that point, but I told the detective Frank shouldn't have a bond.

Why should a murderer have *any* bond in the first place?

I was having chest pains and pains in my jaw and ribs where Frank kicked me. They did more x-rays and said my jaw was bruised and so were my ribs. I told them I was in a lot of pain and it felt like my jaw and ribs were broken. They said everything was fine, and then they told me I was going to have to leave the hospital. My insurance only allowed three days inpatient and I no longer had coverage. I couldn't believe it! After everything I'd been through, now I had to go. I couldn't even bathe myself. I asked if I could go to a nursing home. There were none that would take me without insurance. Three days after the attack, I was packed into a cab and on my way to a shelter.

Nine

SCARFACE

I felt nothing but sadness. I'd been through hell and now I was going with this weird cab driver I knew nothing about. I was suspicious of everyone. I had no idea where I was going. No one had bothered to specifically tell me the name of the shelter and I was on enough painkillers to forget to ask.

The cabbie and I drove in silence, and then he parked at a mechanic's shop. There were few guys working on cars. They were just watching us. I was sitting in the cab wearing my hospital gown and hospital pants. I didn't have a bra or underwear. No one had brought me clothes.

Like something out of a spy thriller, three women came running to the cab, yanked opened the back door and grabbed me, pulling me out. They told me we were going to walk really fast to the shelter down the street. Unbelievable! They were guarding me and running with me. All the mechanics were just gawking at us. I can't imagine what they thought of that scene. I was all stapled and stitched and had both my arms bandaged to the elbows. I had staples and stitches on my face. What a sight! We got to the shelter and they did an intake questionnaire and gave me donated clothes. They showed me my room and coolly shut the door. And that was that. Somehow I thought it would be different. I hoped for someone to spend time with me, to talk to me a little, and offer comfort.

My stomach churned with anxiety; I had no more nurses attending to my care and it seemed I was on my own so quickly. I didn't know what to think. I needed a bath. I hadn't bathed in the three days since the attack. I had dried blood all over, including my hair. My ribs hurt and it still felt like my jaw was broken.

I could hardly move. The trauma to my body followed by three days on my back made my muscles stiff. I just lay down. I pressed my glove-like hands around the pill bottle and clenched the cap in my teeth. Zing! Pain shot up my jaw. I tried again. Finally open, I took some painkillers, which I needed now more than before I chewed open the bottle. Lying there, in this strange place, I just thought about the attack over and over. I couldn't stop it from revolving around my brain.

I slept for a while. When I woke up, I was still in a lot of pain. I needed to take a bath. I went into the bathroom and undressed the best I could without the use of my hands. I was leaning over because my ribs were killing me. I tried to take another pill, but I couldn't open the bottle this time and it fell to the floor. Shaking my head, I just started to cry. "I can't do this!"

I stepped into the bath water. I couldn't get my arms wet, so I kept them out of the water. Gingerly, I wet my hair. I wrestled to open the shampoo with my arms. That didn't work, so I put the shampoo bottle between by arms and tried to open it with my mouth. It wouldn't open. I knew I needed that bath so badly. I couldn't stand being inside my own skin. There's a physical dirtiness that makes you feel ugly—and an emotional dirtiness that makes you feel worthless. I couldn't wash myself of either one.

I put my head down again and cried for all the grief and loss. I felt like giving up. I couldn't do anything for myself and I'd just lost everything. I had no one to help me. Feeling completely broken, and alone, I wanted to die.

Then I got mad. I got out of the tub and struggled to put my clothes back on. I started kicking the bathtub, swore at the toilet, and knocked shampoos and conditioner to the floor. Crying angry and frustrated tears, I left everything the way it was and walked to the office. "I can't do this. I need help. I need a nursing home or someone to help me. I need help with changing, taking a bath, and taking my medicine." Shelter staff said they could not help me with that because they were not a nursing home.

"I think my jaw and ribs are broken," I complained. "I can hardly talk." I told them I needed to go back to the hospital. To calm me, they called the hospital while I was in the office and told them what was going on. They seemed to be arguing back and forth for quite awhile. Who gets Tracy? We can't help her—well, neither can we. The shelter told the hospital I needed a nursing home and possibly had a broken jaw and broken ribs. I needed someone to bathe me. Giving in, the hospital told the shelter to send me back through the emergency room and they would see what they could do. They had a cab driver pick me up and take me back to St. Joseph's. When I got there, I waited about an hour.

After X-rays, they told me my jaw was OK and just sore and that I had a small fracture on my ribs. Good enough shape to leave. "Are you sure, because I can hardly talk? I got punched three times on that side."

They tried to convince me that everything was fine. I desperately wanted to go to a nursing home, but without insurance it was useless. The nurse said they'd keep trying. Finally, they agreed to admit me for one more night. I felt safe there.

"Aren't there nursing homes for people without insurance?" I asked the next day. They suggested I just call some friends.

A nurse called my friend, Martina, who was caring for my kids, though I thought, at the time, they were with my grandparents.

Twenty minutes later she helped me get into her car and told me my kids were at her house. I wasn't ready for them to see me like this. They looked scared when they saw my bandages, staples, and stitches. Cautiously they came over and hugged me. We sat together and talked about everything that had happened.

Martina called two other friends of ours and the three of them bathed me, gently sponging off cakes of bloody hair and carefully combing out the knots. It soothed and calmed my frayed nerves and for the first time in days I didn't feel alone.

Over the next few days, more friends came to see me while I was staying at Martina's house. Telling my story became part of the healing process. We spoke quietly and often with tears. I was in some sort of surreal existence. I remembered so clearly what I'd gone through and still couldn't believe it had happened. At the same time, it made so much sense. Frank had always told me he'd kill me if I ever tried to leave him. I knew it was more than a threat. Now it had happened and I'd lived through it. But I lost my mother. I was grieving and my children were suffering from the loss and the aftershock of what I'd been through. Each of them had experienced trauma. What Chelsea experienced was different from what Alex had, and they had different ways of dealing with their shock.

Since Martina didn't have a car, it was going to be difficult for me to get to appointments. We decided I would stay with her sister-in-law and my children would stay with her. I didn't want to be separated from them at a time when we really needed to be close to each other. But I had to be realistic. I couldn't care for them; I couldn't even care for myself.

Martina's sister-in-law lived well outside the Phoenix city limits.

Chapter Nine | Scarface

Their home, in a remote, rural area, was large enough for me to have a bedroom to myself. The privacy did me good. Sometimes you don't want people to see you cry. As awkward as it was to stay with people I hardly knew, they welcomed me with opened arms.

Nightmares woke me up every time I tried to sleep. At night, I would sit outside and watch the stars, smoking cigarettes. But Frank was everywhere and I was haunted and terrified. I was sure he was behind every tree, looking for the perfect moment when he could finish the killing he'd threatened so many times. Every night noise made me jump and I'd run back to the safety of the house.

After staying at Martina's awhile, my children went to my grandparents' for a few more days. Then they came to stay with me at the friend's house. We shared a room, which helped all of us feel more secure and less lonely.

The day came for my mother's funeral. Getting ready made me edgy and scared. I was taking pills for my pain, but they didn't help my nerves. The pills kept me on the fence balancing somewhere between minimum awareness and complete lethargy. I felt out of myself when I was on the pills, but the pain was so overbearing. If I didn't take them, every fiber of my body screamed. My nerve endings were cut and daily rituals, like showering, felt like fire. I knew I'd be asked a lot of questions about the attack. I felt sick at heart and guilty that a fight with Frank caused my mother's death. And I knew Glenn, my brother, would be there. I hadn't seen him in years. The prison was allowing him to come to the funeral, but he would be in handcuffs and ankle shackles the whole time.

I went to the funeral with Chelsea and some of my friends. Everyone was crying and in shock, no one more so than me. It was terrible for my grandparents and my daughter. And as I predicted, everyone was asking me questions about what had happened and how I felt. Some wanted to know what I thought of the whole thing. What did they expect? I was angry—very, *very* angry. I answered their questions the best I could, feeling comforted knowing they were all friends and family anyway. I wish I'd known, at the time, how some of my comments, overheard by others, would be misinterpreted and used against me in the months to come.

The doctor I worked for was there and I was surprised to see him, just that he would take the time to come and support me. He'd been sympathetic the whole time I was in the hospital and supportive of me leaving my job to recover. We spoke for a few minutes before the funeral and I think he may have felt badly. Frank had come to the clinic to argue with me only a couple hours before the attack. It was even caught on the clinic's security video tape, but no one had been able to stop him or help me during the argument at work.

With Glenn in handcuffs and shackles and me in stitches, staples, and bandages up to my elbows, I'm sure we looked like quite a pair. Without our hands, we could barely touch each other. Chest-to-chest, we kissed each other's cheeks like movie stars at a cocktail party.

I sat between Glenn and Chelsea. My grandparents sat on Chelsea's other side. She was crying so hard and my heart broke for her. It's too much for a girl of eight to go through. Everyone's heart ached in his or her own way. Glenn grieved for our mother and the time he'd lost being with her because he was in prison. My grandparents grieved the loss of a daughter who'd had a difficult life and should have outlived them. Aunts and uncles grieved for a lost sister. And I grieved for the mother I had tried so hard to have a relationship with. She was the one I'd shared raising my children with, and the friend I was getting to know. My mother's last unselfish act was to protect me, as only a mother can, and as a result she lost her life. How would we get over that?

My mother had wished to be cremated and so she was. A month later, my uncle took her ashes to California and threw them into the Pacific, just as she had wanted.

My brother got up and talked at the funeral about our mother. He said, "Thank you, Mom, for everything. You have always been there for me when I had nowhere to go. When I had no food, you fed me. I love you, Mom, and I will see you real soon."

I couldn't stop crying.

After the funeral, I hugged my brother goodbye. Only close family could go near him. With handcuffs and shackles, he couldn't hug back. The rest of us went to my grandparents' house. There were just a few of us over there to eat dinner. We all sat around and talked about what happened. Curiosity got the best of everyone and they wanted me to take my bandages off so they could see my stab wounds. I was really out of it from my painkillers. It was like some sort of freak show. Chelsea stayed behind with my grandmother. I went back to Martina's friend's home where Alex was waiting. A couple days later, my Chelsea came too. We stayed for about a week.

I kept calling my landlord to tell him I wanted to move out of my townhouse. He was completely unsympathetic to what had happened and wouldn't let me out of my lease or I'd owe him four months' rent. Total jerk. At $950 a month times four it would be $3,800 and I would lose my $1,200 deposit. He was going to make me stay there or my credit would be screwed for a long time. He expected me to replace the carpet that had been soaked with blood and cut to pieces by the police.

About a week before I went back home to live, I had to go to the house to get clothes for the kids and myself. My grandmother had a set of keys and gave them to me so I could go with a friend.

My house looked like something out of a slasher movie. Bloody footprints left trails from the kitchen to the foyer. More prints had gone from the porch, to the street, to the neighbor's garage. Everywhere beyond our home, the blood trail had been washed away. But inside told the story.

The carpet was cut out in various places all over the house.

We walked around in my room and there was a lot of carpet cut out, like backwards patchwork. I flashed back and saw myself struggling to survive the torturous hours. I zoned out for a minute as I mentally lay on the floor willing myself not to breathe so Frank would believe I was dead. I could hear Alex's little voice; "Do you want me to shoot Dada?"

It was like *he* was in there. There was still blood on the ceiling fan. Blood sprays everywhere. I'd been on the floor by the Arcadia door when Frank sliced the back of my neck. The door still had blood on the blinds. I started to feel panicky; I was getting dizzy and my stomach heaved. I needed to leave. I grabbed for summer clothes and fled.

On the way back to the home where I was staying, we stopped at a Circle K convenience store and everyone was looking at me and asking what happened to my face and arms. It made me so self-conscious. I told them my husband stabbed me several times. We stopped at other places, for shampoo and necessities, and people recognized me from being on the news. "That was *you*?" I was telling my story over and over again.

Ten

PTSD

After another week, I knew it was time to go back to my own home. I didn't want to. I wasn't ready and probably never would be. I was so scared to go back there, but I had no choice.

It felt like my mom and Frank were still there. Their presence was everywhere and I think the kids felt it as much as I did. It was just a weird, unreal feeling. It was so hard to go to bed that first night. If I closed my eyes even for a second, I imagined all sorts of bad things happening. The three of us slept together, and even though they were children, my kids comforted me with their warmth and soft breathing.

In the morning, I went upstairs and started to go through my mom's room. It was eerie, like being in some forbidden place snooping in someone's personal belongings. My mom had pictures of herself and my dad together next to the bed. My father had been deceased for thirty years already. It was weird to see pictures of my dad next to her bed. I couldn't remember the last time I'd seen any of him.

I guess she'd just gotten the pictures out a day or two before the attack because I'd never seen them there before. I sat there for a while, wondering why she had pictures like that next to her bed. Why did she get them out now? Did she somehow sense something? Was it a premonition or her growing depression gaining on her?

Sorting through my mother's closet, I thought she was watching me, because she used to always get mad at me when I went through her closet to borrow something. Any minute now she'd snap, "What are you looking for? Ask me if you want to wear something of mine!"

Every little noise made me jump. The attack was going over and over in my head, my built-in instant replay that I couldn't shut off. I was scared in there, thinking if Frank was to come in I would be trapped, alone upstairs, and I would, for sure, be dead. It took me two hours to go through my mother's closet. Just sorting clothes, choosing the things I was going to keep.

I continued to work around the house. A meticulous housekeeper by nature, I took buckets of water from room to room and scrubbed the evidence of my own suffering. I cleaned walls, fans, and railings. I picked up bloody clothes from the floor and hoped to bring back some sort of order and peace. The forensics team had cleaned a little bit, but there were still painful reminders everywhere.

How was I going to pay the rent in a couple months? I was OK financially for about a month because someone had set up a fund through Bank One for me. Friends and generous strangers had donated whatever they could ... The bar where I worked had a car wash to raise money for me too, and they also had a canned food collection for me. I had plenty of food. To this day, there are still pictures of the car wash on the walls at the bar. I had enough money for rent, my car payment, and the electric bill that was already a couple months past due.

But I had to decide what I was going to do next. I couldn't work. I had slashes all over my face, a long cut to the back of my neck, cuts on my legs, and I'd lost partial use of my left thumb. Whether as a dancer or a medical assistant, I wasn't ready for the public. I wasn't ready, physically or emotionally. I felt ugly and scarred. Overwhelmed, I was still in shock and could barely function day-to-day. Chelsea, Alex, and I were all going to counseling. I applied for government financial aid.

In the meantime, Frank continued to write letters and send them to my grandparents' address. In one, dated September 1, 2001, Frank told Alex how much he loved and missed him and that they had a "special bond together that bond will keep us knowing each other … one day, Son we will be together." I felt Frank was trying to make me feel sorry for him—keeping him away from his son. It seemed he wanted me to drop the charges and we could forget the whole thing.

Within a few months I started to feel really, really sick. There was a weakness and nausea I couldn't stop. I went to the doctor and told him the whole story of what happened, and that I'd had a blood transfusion. He took blood samples. About three days later, he called me back to his office. There I got the news; I had Hepatitis C. "Oh. My God!" I told him. "My mom had Hepatitis C. So maybe I got it when Frank used the same knife on her that he used on me."

The doctor advised me to get my hospital records to see if I had Hepatitis C when I was admitted to the hospital the night of the attack. The records showed I hadn't had it. Hepatitis C usually takes a couple months to show in your blood and its symptoms to appear.

But I also thought I may have gotten it through the transfusion. The doctor was making referrals to send me to a specialist. In the meantime, I applied for disability because I was really sick, my face was messed up, and I couldn't use my hands. I was still having a lot of surgery on my face and hands. Every night, I put Mederma® and Preparation H® on my facial scars. Doctors performed microdermabrasion, where they'd basically sand my skin. It was painful and left my face red for days between each treatment. I was putting everything I could think of on my face because I did not want Frank to win. He wanted to make me too ugly for anyone to want. No way. Someday, I'd be me again. And the only scars would be on the inside.

I applied for disability Social Security Income, SSI. About two months later, they approved me and I got back pay and was approved money for my son to see a counselor. He was going through a lot, too, and had been diagnosed with Post Traumatic Stress Disorder, or PTSD. I was so happy I was going to have some income so I could survive while I got through this Hepatitis C and got my life back on track.

I was watching TV one night and was startled to hear, "Breaking news," a newscaster said, "A prisoner has escaped the Madison Street Jail. He's described as five feet eleven inches tall, Hispanic, short dark hair, brown eyes, medium build."

"Oh, my God, it's Frank!" Panicked, I got down on the floor and called 9-1-1 and told them that Frank had killed my mom and tried to kill me. He'd just escaped from jail and was after me. It was on the news. I thought he was in the house.

The dispatcher asked me for more information and I ran outside carrying the phone with me. I didn't want to be stuck in the house again getting tortured. I figured I was safer outside where there were more places to run and possible witnesses. She kept me on the phone. I begged her, "Please don't get off the phone until we find out if it was him!"

The kids were asleep. I didn't know how to keep them safe. She found out who the missing prisoner was and it wasn't Frank. I whimpered, "Are you sure?" I felt like I was losing my mind. I realized I, too, had PTSD.

The next day I told my counselor, and my kids' counselors what had happened. They said we needed to move out. We couldn't heal in that house of memories. I told them my landlord wouldn't let me out of the lease. The counselor called the landlord and laid it on the line. I talked to him again too. The creep wouldn't budge. He belligerently said I could not move out or I would lose my $1,200 deposit. I moved anyway and lost the money.

I found another place that was a little less expensive than where I'd been that I could afford on SSI and my kids and I moved in within a few days. The doctor prescribed injections for the Hepatitis. He said I'd be very sick for a year. I would lose my hair, become anorexic and psychotic. I decided to wait until the criminal trial was over before I would start injections. I needed the injections, but I also needed to be able to think. It would take every ounce of strength to see Frank again.

Eleven

CAN YOU HEAR ME?

**Article for Kerry G. Wangberg's
FOR THE STATE "WHY WE DO WHAT WE DO" section**
By Sandra Hunter 448884v1

On August 10, 2000, Tracy Stombres predicted her husband would kill them. He almost killed her that afternoon, strangling her neck with his bare hands. He pressed his fingers into her eyes trying to gouge them out. She tried to reason with him, pleaded for him not to hurt her with their baby in the house. He told her he didn't care, he'd kill them all. As she spoke to the 9-1-1 operator about what happened, her voice shook, breaking into choked sobs. Several times during the course of the call, she stated that he would kill her, at once sounding so certain, and at the same time sounding so unwilling to believe it would ever come to that.

That afternoon was only one moment in time, one attack of many during the course of their marriage. Tracy struggled between the fear of staying with him and the fear of leaving. Officers encouraged her to get an order of protection. She told them it would do no good against a bullet. Prosecutors in Glendale had charged him with assault and criminal damage from an earlier attack. She did not appear for court and the charges were dismissed. The City of Phoenix Prosecutor's Office charged him with assault for the attack from August 2000. In May 2001, Tracy decided that the fear of staying was now greater than her fear of leaving. She separated from him and began to meet with the Phoenix Prosecutor's Office. Almost as soon as she had left, however, Tracy was sucked back in. Her husband moved back into her house and into their lives.

On August 1, 2001, almost one year to the day from her fateful prediction to 9-1-1, her husband struck. Instead of a bullet, he used a knife. He stabbed Tracy on her face, neck, back, and arms. Tracy's mother tried to intervene, so he stabbed her as well. As he dragged Tracy upstairs, she watched her mother stumble out of the house. Tracy turned all her attention to staying alive. She played dead. For three hours, she lay on the floor, hoping for rescue. Each time he walked by her, he'd stab her again. When officers finally came, they found Tracy alive, along with her two year old son, who had witnessed everything. Tracy's mother did not survive. She had made it as far as the garage before dying from the loss of blood.

On August 10, 2000, Tracy Stombres predicted her husband would kill them. He partly succeeded. And even though he is currently in custody for murder and attempted murder, Tracy is still scared he'll come back to finish her off. Let us all hope he does not succeed in fulfilling the rest of her prediction.

Chapter Eleven | Can You Hear Me?

The time had come to face Frank in the criminal trial. A year had gone by since the attack. The trial was scheduled to begin on July, 30, 2002, but was delayed until August first, and would last a couple weeks. I was going to have to sit in the same room with him day after day, and I wasn't so sure how I could do that.

Ironically, and painfully, exactly one year from the attack, we were assembled in court. I, for one, felt like I was fighting for my life again. I was fighting for justice and emotional compensation—and I was powerless.

Before the trial began, I had to see the state's prosecutor, Susan Brnovich, several times for preparation. We discussed what questions would be asked of him and of me, who the witnesses were, and so on. She told me not to get a lawyer because she was the assigned state prosecutor. So my grandmother and I didn't get one. She also told me that when the news reported the incident on TV, Frank's ex-girlfriend, Jody, called silent witness and reported that Frank was using a fake name. I'd known this before, but only because Frank's stepfather adopted him. I also knew he had two Social Security numbers. He tried to go to jail with the name that had no criminal record until she called silent witness.

It took a lot of bravery on Jody's part to come forward. She had the sense of doing the right thing. The prosecutor called Jody in and asked for the details of her relationship with Frank—and how it was relevant to my case. She had dated him for a year and a half and experienced a lot of violence in the relationship. She said he struck her several times. Once he burnt her with a cigarette and kicked her down the stairs. When she attempted to leave him, Frank barricaded the door in the house so she couldn't get out. Then he choked her to the point of unconsciousness in his bedroom. He tried to sexually assault her. When she woke up, he had a knife to her chest. He didn't cut her, but he made cutting motions, leaving marks, like his initials. He told Jody, "If I can't have you, no one can." Everything Frank did to her was so much like what he'd done to me over the years. How could she describe it so accurately if it wasn't true? When he went to jail for that attack, he wrote to her and sweet-talked her. Intimidated, she changed her story to the police and dropped the charges. The prosecutor told her she could get in trouble for the past perjury. This did nothing to help a woman who had so generously felt she needed to speak up now on behalf of another woman.

She said she was confused because he was so sweet sometimes; it was he was like two different people, and she said she still had a few letters that showed the tendencies of two personalities. Jody explained to Susan that she would do anything to help and would be willing to testify in the criminal trial.

Sitting in the same room with Frank was terrifying. I could just see him jumping from his chair to attack me—and these people would have no way to stop him. Frank just stared at me with evil in his eyes.

The jury instructions were an inch and a half thick. So many details! The second day the jury received a new packet, which was just as big as the first. For some reason, the judge would not allow me to see it, nor would anyone explain exactly why they had new instructions. What had changed? Why? That was the beginning of many rulings that favored the defendant—leaving me in the dark, excluded from my own fight. One of the instructions served to the jury was that they must not consider any statement made by the defendant to a law enforcement officer. It read, "Unless you determine that beyond a reasonable doubt the defendant made the statement voluntarily." I couldn't understand this because in the police report all the officers were people Frank had talked to right away before thinking of a prepared defense for trial. The instructions also said, "You must not consider a prior conviction as evidence of the crime for which the defendant is now on trial." In other words, the jury would never be made aware that there were any previous assault charges or convictions—ever. In their eyes,

Chapter Eleven | Can You Hear Me?

Frank was a squeaky clean guy who'd never hurt a fly. The numerous attacks on me and time served, the attacks and time served for his assault on Jody, and his previous time for other crimes flat didn't exist! The jury was supposed to make an informed decision with no information at all. I was stunned at this violation of justice, and the worst part was that there was more to come.

These instructions pertained to the charges of second degree murder of my mother, manslaughter by "sudden quarrel or heat of passion," and attempted first degree murder on me. Next was aggravated assault on me, then kidnapping of me and my mom. Why jurors could not consider prior convictions of evidence, I just couldn't understand. It also said for the jury not to do research or make any investigation whatsoever about the case on their own. I wondered, "Why not?" And in order to find him guilty of second degree murder, they must prove all three charges; that the defendant did it intentionally number one; number two that he knew he would cause death or serious physical injury, number three that he recklessly engaged in conduct that created risk of death. So they had to find all three for a guilty verdict. I was there, in that house of bloodshed and misery. I knew he was guilty of all three counts.

With the charge of attempted murder on me, they also needed to prove three things. One, he acted to cause death; two, he knew that he would act to cause death—"Aren't you dead yet, bitch?"— and three, he acted with premeditation.

For the aggravated assault, they only had to prove two things. One that he acted with intent knowingly or recklessly caused physical injury to another person; and two, the defendant used a dangerous instrument.

For him to claim self-defense, they had to prove that in his situation he would have believed that deadly physical force was necessary to protect himself from harm.

The instructions were ridiculous. I was being set up to lose from the start. I believed Frank's charm and charisma duped the judge into protecting him from his true past ever being known. The jury was in the dark and would stay that way. The judge would see to that, I felt. Basically, it was Frank's word against my mom's, and my mom was no longer around. No one would listen to me and I wasn't allowed a voice. Susan Brnovich was limited in her abilities to prosecute with so much information prohibited. Jody would not be allowed to testify. Judge's orders. That testimony, so similar and so critical, was lost to us. We needed it! I was crushed. Frank looked smug and pleased with himself as he sat in the defendant's chair wearing a crisp suit and tie—on loan from the personal wardrobe of the presiding judge himself.

Of the 700 police photographs, a mere sixteen were allowed as evidence in the trial. For hours, the court and the attorneys debated about what we could and could not say. One of the things Frank's public defender wanted to bring up was all my past charges. But we could not raise the attempted murder incident with Jody, nearly identical to my own, that was from seven years prior. My personal credibility was being filleted in front of everyone. Frank's would remain untainted. I just didn't get it. And still, no one would speak up for me.

During the trial, I felt like I was the one in trouble or had done something wrong. We couldn't talk about his three prior felony convictions; a robbery, two aggravated assaults. There were also various misdemeanors.

"Are you listening to me, Ms. Stombres?" The judge ordered me. "Make sure you don't talk, you don't talk about these things at all. Don't try to blurt it out in any way. Or talk about any past abuse. Do you understand me, Ms. Stombres?" No, I didn't understand why he would not let me talk about it. Why can't they, the jury, be allowed to know?

"Don't testify about the fight or assaultive behavior by Frank." If I can't testify about that, I thought, then, what are we here for?

Chapter Eleven | Can You Hear Me?

The entire long and draining day consisted of nothing but jury instructions. How could they remember all that? Why was every point debated by the attorneys? Endless.

When I came home, I was told a letter had arrived at my grandparents' house from Frank. It was addressed to Alex again. The same stuff. I love you, Son, I miss you. The following day I told the prosecutor about the letter. It was tearing my grandparents apart to receive jail letters from their daughter's killer at their home. An incessant and painful reminder in the midst of the trial, and they didn't need the insult. Ms. Brnovich pacified me, assuring me she would ask the judge to direct Frank to stop his letter writing to my relatives. At 10:00 a.m. on August 2, 2002, we reconvened for the second day of trial.

I was called to the stand, and they swore me in. The prosecuting attorney for the state, Susan Brnovich, asked how long I was married, about the kids, and other basic questions. Over and over I answered questions that didn't seem relevant. She asked about our separation—when we got back together, how Frank had my son in Texas, and how I let him come back because I missed my son. Ms. Brnovich asked me about Cory, the guy who helped me move. I explained that he was just a friend. We talked about the layout of the house and the floor plan. Ms. Brnovich's purpose was to allow the jury to get to know me, as a wife, a mother, someone who cares deeply about the welfare of her children and who had tried, for years, as I had done, to survive and persevere during an abusive marriage. Mr. Canby, the defense attorney, wanted to paint a different picture. He wanted the jury to presume I was unfaithful and a difficult wife. Frank, Mr. Canby alleged, was the victim here.

We led into the point when the attack started. How Frank met Cory and how Frank asked me if I'd had sex with Cory. As evidence, they brought in video tape from the security camera at the medical clinic where I worked. It showed Frank coming to my work hours before the attack. On the video tape, he was getting really mad at me in the waiting room. He was flailing his hands and gesticulating wildly. You couldn't hear him, on tape, but you could see him arguing with me. He was yelling at me about Cory, demanding to know if I'd slept with him.

In the video, I could be seen wearing my clinic scrubs and tennis shoes, my hair woven into a long French braid. This was an important piece of footage because you can see Frank's actions and more importantly, because later evidence showed my hair cut off in photos, but we couldn't find the actual braid. Frank may have flushed it down the toilet. The police only found handfuls of my hair. The police report taken the day of the attack indicated evidence items #5, #6, and #7, all being hair found in various parts of the house.

We got into questions about the attack. They showed me pictures of my house from the sixteen photos allowed as evidence. The prosecution asked me what happened in each part of the house as I gave them a virtual tour, using the photos and retelling the horror. In the year leading to this trial, many people had asked me what happened. The practice had been good for me, giving me the opportunity to release trauma from my system, and yet it was nothing like the pain of reliving and retelling in front of my grandparents, Frank, and the strangers in the jury box. I cried when I saw pictures of the bloody carpet where I'd seen my mom holding her arms in the air, kneeling, crying, "I'm bleeding!" That was the last time I heard her voice and saw her alive.

Sometimes when you feel a lot of emotions at once, you don't know what to feel—take your pick. I was sad, mad, and scared. I was overwhelmed. The prosecutor asked if I was taken to the hospital and how many surgeries I'd had. She asked about the pain I still had in different parts of my body from damaged nerves and scars. She asked about the surgeries I was still having. They showed different pictures of the wounds on my face, hands, and head, all nicely stapled and stitched. Stab wound by stab wound. The prosecutor explained to the judge that these pictures were cleaned up because they were taken hours after the surgery and not immediately after the ambulance arrived.

She showed photos of my mother and asked if I recognized the picture. It was a heartrending picture of my mother. She was laid out on a gurney in the morgue with blood from head to toe; her head was turned to the side and her eyes open and glazed. The knife hole in her neck was dark, raw, and angry looking. That's when I broke down. The people in the courtroom gasped at the graphic pictures.

I explained how I bled on my pillow for weeks after the attack because the surgeon never checked my head. I had been cut all over my scalp. Blood leaked from tiny knife wounds all over my head. I didn't realize what was causing the continuous bleeding until much later. To this day, my head itches from the scars.

Ms. Brnovich showed pictures of my nose. I explained that those were pictures taken after they reattached my nose from nostril to tip. I had to explain each cut on my body, taking the courtroom back through the experience with me.

It was time for cross-examination by Frank's public defender. He asked me really stupid questions. He asked about Cory—if I was having sex with Cory while Frank was in Texas. I explained, again, we were friends. As if any form of a relationship, with anyone, gave Frank license to kill. One of the toughest perceptions an abused woman deals with is that it's "her fault," a double standard that any behavior in her part is justification for abuse. Canby was exacerbating that belief and feeding it to the jury. I didn't understand what difference it made. What I'd done, or who I was with while Frank was in Texas, was irrelevant. It didn't give him the right to kill my mom or to try to kill me. No one ever asked Frank if he'd had extramarital sex while he was in Texas, or at any other time during our marriage.

On the next day of the trial, the first witness was Officer James Ray. They asked him about that day, August 1, 2001. He said I was still getting attacked while all the officers were outside. When he called the house, a male answered the phone, and confirmed himself as Frank. The officers asked if everything was OK. Frank would not answer at first, then started to cry. He said, "She's been cheating on me." The officer told him he needed to come out of the house and talk to them. Frank said, "I don't want to see a cop and I better not see a cop."

Officer Ray's report, typed the evening of the attack, states:
> "While en route, I used my cell phone to contact the complainant. She advised me that the problem was at her granddaughter, and she gave me the home number of (number was here). She gave me the granddaughter's name of Tracy and the husband as Frank. (Approximate 20 second phone call).
>
> Then telephoned the house. A male answered the phone and I asked if he was Frank. He answered, "Yes". I identified myself as Officer Ray, Phoenix Police Department, and asked if everything was OK in the house. He began to cry and I asked again. There was a long pause, and I then asked why he wouldn't answer the door when the officer knocked {author's note: another officer (Perry) was already on the scene}. He stated, "She's been cheating on me." I asked him to go outside and speak to the officer on scene. At this time, he stated "I don't want to shoot a cop, I better not see one." Radio was advised.
>
> Upon arrival at the house at 1725 hours, I was still on the phone with Frank. He wasn't giving out much information, but informed me that his son was in the

apartment with him. Officer Perry and I contacted Officer Oehler (badge number) and then took a position directly across from the front door of 7XXX North 19th Avenue. We were in the covered carport at 7XXX North 19th Lane that contained a silver Saturn.

Officer Perry began observing the front door area, while I remained further into the carport on the cell phone. I spoke to Frank about coming out to speak with us, and assured him that he wouldn't be harmed. We went back and forth on the phone for several minutes. He would listen, but not say much, and then hang up. About three to four minutes into the conversation, he went to the front door and opened it. I could hear Officer Perry yelling at him to come out and give up. After re-entering the house, Officer Perry turned around to face me. He looked past me at the wall and said, "What's that?" I was on the passenger side of the vehicle by the front door. I moved towards the front hood, and observed a large amount of blood on the wall. While following it down to the ground, saw a Hispanic female wearing a black tank top and red shorts lying on the carport floor. There was blood everywhere on her face, neck and clothes. A large pool of blood had pooled around her head. The Hispanic female was lying on her back. The head was north and feet south. Hands were along her sides and her face was facing east. I stood by her for approximately thirty seconds and saw no movement. Her chest never rose or fell, and there was no body movement. I had Officer Perry visually see the body and then informed radio.

I telephoned Frank and asked what he had done to

his wife. He would not answer. I told him that I had a Hispanic female with injuries and he stated, "That's not my wife, that's my mother-in-law." He asked if she was OK and I informed him that she needed medical help. {Ray testified this was done so as not to increase Frank's agitation}. We told him on the phone and by yelling, that he needed to come out unarmed, and give up, so we could get help for her. Frank refused and stated over the phone, 'I got nothing to lose'. He then hung up."

To this day, I don't understand why Frank didn't get charged with threatening an officer and resisting arrest. Next, a detective got on the stand. He was the negotiator. He was authorized by the FBI to teach throughout the state. This detective said Frank wouldn't answer the phone when he called back. The officer had to go over to our window to ask Frank to please pick up the phone so all the people, the neighbors and bystanders wouldn't hear the conversation. Finally, Frank answered the phone and asked the officer, "How come you haven't moved my mother-in-law yet?" Apparently Frank could see through my son's bedroom window that she was in the carport across the street. The detective placated Frank, saying, "We moved her and she's on her way to the hospital." The Detective was trying to minimize her injuries. Then the officer on the stand said that Frank had told him that he was confused and didn't want to come out of the house and he was sorry for what had happened but things got out of hand. He said his mother-in-law tried to step in on the fight and the next thing he knew he grabbed the knife and cut her. These were his words to the negotiator and the negotiator had it on paper.

They called the sergeant on to the stand. The same one that had gotten the backboard for my mother to carry her to the ambulance. The sergeant testified that he and the van driver had to put on body armor to protect themselves. They loaded my mother onto

Chapter Eleven | Can You Hear Me?

a backboard and carried her while crouching behind the slowly moving van until they got a block away. They left her by a fire hydrant until a firefighter could check her out.

I don't know how long she was there that evening, but months after the attack there was still blood on the ground by that hydrant. My friends and family often lay flowers there, and decorate the hydrant, to memorialize her.

They called Officer Spitler on the stand. He'd arrived at the scene when it was all ending. He said Frank was unemotional. He's the officer that found me and my son. This officer explained how he saw my legs sticking out upstairs just beyond the bed. I was barely moving and there was blood all over my face and body. He explained how my nose was hanging sideways. He testified about the firemen and EMTs who came to help me. They continued to show pictures while he was on the stand and asked him questions.

Officer Spitler said that from the time Frank walked out until the time he found me two minutes had gone by. "Okay", Brnovich said, "And while she was being treated how long did it take for the paramedics to get there?" Spitler responded, "Paramedics arrived and started treating Tracy at 18:29, which is 6:29 p.m. And that was six minutes after we made entry."

"Okay. And what did Tracy say about her mother?"

"She said the defendant stabbed her mother in the – I believe it was the kitchen area (refers to his notes) stabbed her mother in the living room area and that she was referring to what she said about her mother or both of them."

"Did she continue to explain where she was cut?"

"Yeah. She said she was stabbed."

"Objection, Your Honor." Candy interrupted.

"On the basis of hearsay?" asked the Judge.

Susan Brnovich answered, "Excited utterance."

At the side bar Candy explained to the Judge, "I think, if I'm not mistaken, excited utterance would have to be close to the time of the event that she is describing, that we're talking about now with this testimony about an hour and fifteen minutes from the first call in, so obviously I think that's late."

The Judge said, "Okay, I'm denying ... I'm sustaining the objection. It does not appear to be that close to the time to when the injuries were inflicted here to qualify as an excited utterance. There was a lot of testimony about the standoff or the time consumed with the defendant refusing to come out, and on that basis I don't find its excited utterance. The objection is sustained."

By saying, "excited utterance," Susan Brnovich had suggested the legal term that ultimately had valuable testimony disallowed. Evidently neither she, nor Officer Spitler, were willing to argue, on my behalf, that my first words to the first person I saw upon my rescue were key testimony. Was anyone going to fight for my rights here? Here's how it stood: the officers arrived at my house at 1705. Two *hours* later, at 1825, they made entry. Two *minutes* later I was found and spoke my first possible words to someone other than Frank. And they weren't calling it excited utterance. Answer me this: how is that not "close in time"?

In Canby's cross-examination, they debated the point about blood on the walls going up the staircase. Canby was saying that it came from me being carried down the stairs by the firefighters. He contended that there was no blood on the stairs before that because I had gone upstairs willingly. But the blood was already on the walls when they loaded me into body sling that covered my whole body.

Canby asked the officer, "Did the little boy, Alex, look upset or traumatized?" Frank's lawyer had talked about the fact that my son was laughing on the phone with 9-1-1 when they kept calling the house. I wanted to scream, "He was only two-and-a-half years old! No one knows if Frank was tickling him or doing anything to make him sound happy!"

Chapter Eleven | Can You Hear Me?

Next they called the paramedic to the stand. Like everyone else, they asked him questions and showed him pictures. He said the SWAT team brought a middle-aged woman to the paramedics and she was "obviously deceased." He said it was so obvious that all they did was put a sheet over her and leave her on the street by a fire hydrant. He also said he stuck around about an hour before he got to go into the house. They asked him if he noticed anything unusual. He said yes, "There was a lot of blood everywhere on the walls and the staircase." He recalled he'd never seen anything like that before in his career as a paramedic. Blood was on the walls, blinds, ceiling fan, everywhere.

They asked him to describe all my injuries. He explained how I had a subcutaneous air or fluid escaping from my neck. It was so obvious that he was very concerned about life threatening injuries. He also explained avulsion to the nose and they asked him to define it. He said an actual part of the nose was missing and he said it's not like a cut, "It's like the whole tip was gone." He described how they gave me IV fluids on the scene and tried to stop the blood the best they could.

They gave the members of the jury the opportunity to ask questions on paper that were submitted to the judge, but the judge could choose whether to have them answered, depending on what he thought of the question. One question was the response of the lights and sirens; what code they were, seemingly to understand the gravity of my situation. The paramedic said, "Yes, we turned the lights and sirens on." He said my blood pressure was way down. A juror asked if I would have died, and he said, "Yes, she would have been dead if it had been another five to ten minutes."

He said my blood pressure went really high in the ambulance. They assumed it was adrenaline from finally being out of the house and being rushed to the hospital.

Then the attorneys called my grandmother, my mother's mother, to the stand. They asked her questions about my mother's childhood. We were beginning to get used to the routine of questioning before getting down to why we were really there. Finally, they asked my grandmother about the day of the attack. She explained that Frank sounded agitated, that day, when he asked her to call his mother in Texas. My grandmother didn't know what was going on so she called his mom. Frank's mother called her back about twenty minutes later and told my grandmother to call the ambulance because, "Frank cut your granddaughter." Before my grandparents went to the house to see what was going on, my grandmother called the house, but at first Frank wouldn't answer the phone. Finally, he did answer, and my grandmother asked, "Where's Vina?" He said, "She's lying on the ground outside." My grandmother started to cry on the stand when she retold the story. She told the jury she asked Frank, "What do you mean she's laying on the ground?" But Frank had hung up.

When she and my grandfather got to the house, they couldn't find a place to park. People were everywhere. She went under the yellow caution tape and the officers grabbed her and my grandfather and escorted them to a rescue van. She explained how after a while they brought Alex to the van. He had one of the squirt guns in his hand. The same as he'd shown me when he offered to shoot Dada. She said the police told her Chelsea was at McDonald's. They finally let them all go, my grandparents, daughter, and son, and they were going to the hospital to see me.

At last they let her off the stand and called Cory to testify. Cory confirmed that we were friends. He said he didn't start dating me until after my mother passed away. He said he also knew when Frank came back to live with me, but he'd stayed in contact with my mother to make sure Frank wasn't going to beat me. Cory told the court how he went to the house on August first to borrow $20 from my mother. When he got there Frank came out of the house and looked at Cory "crazy." They started to talk and they got into Frank's truck to get something to eat. Cory said Frank was adamant on finding out if we had sex. Cory described for the jury, "'No', I told him, but Frank wouldn't stop asking." Every time Cory said no, Frank would think of another way to ask. They went into the house and Frank announced towards Mother's room, "Cory's here" and they went upstairs together, but my mom would not open the door. "I guess she was scared not knowing what Frank would do." Cory said when he was leaving that Frank started to talk to him about church and God. Cory offered Frank his pager number in case Frank ever wanted to ask him more questions. But once he had it, Frank repeatedly paged Cory all afternoon, asking, "Did you ever kiss my wife or have sex with her?"

Cory described how he felt that day. After he heard about the attack, he drove to our house. He saw the cloth-covered body on the sidewalk. He lost it. He climbed back into his Jeep but couldn't drive. He had to call someone for a ride. He thought it was my body the whole time. Around midnight that night, he got another phone call. A defiant male voice, "How do you like your bitch now?"

The kitchen where the fight started.

My mom's and Frank's footprints in mom's blood.

The blood from Frank cutting my neck and other lacerations.

Mom's bloody handprint and pool of blood where she passed away trying to get help at the neighbor's house.

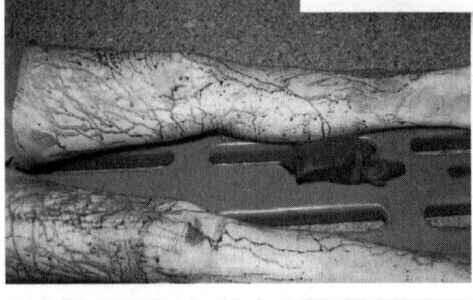
My mother's blood-covered legs.

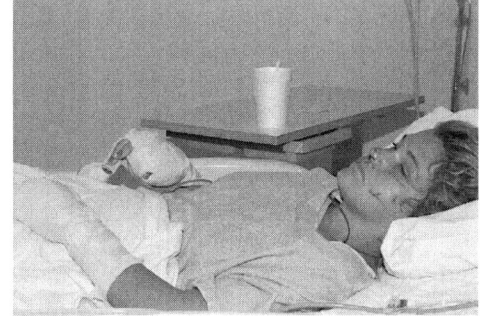

Me in the hospital after emergency plastic surgery.

Where Frank tried to cut off my head.

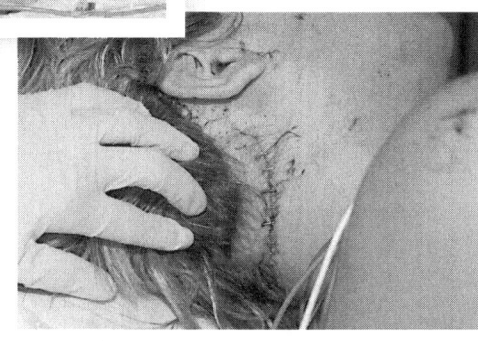

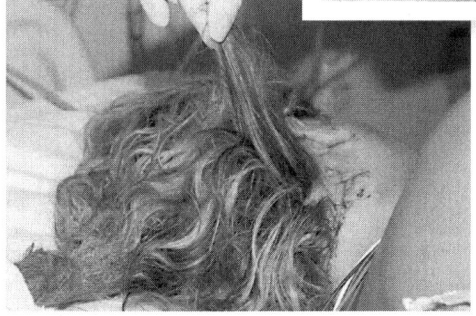

The knotted remains of hair after Frank cut off my French braid.

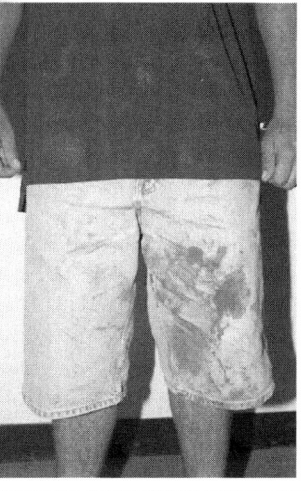

Frank's shorts with my blood from him straddling me.

My mother's covered body where they moved her to the street.

Twelve

COURT INJUSTICE

The next day was August 2, 2002. Ordered by the court not to speak and not to comment, I was helplessly dependant on the skills of the state's prosecution.

The state called Detective D'Aguanno, a twenty-six year veteran with the Phoenix Police Department. He explained that he'd interviewed the primary victim in this case, an assault victim. He'd also interviewed my grandmother, Lillian Calderon. After the interviews, he'd gone to the police station and interviewed the suspect, Frank Gomez.

"While you were with Mr. Gomez, did you notice any injuries to Gomez's face?" asked the prosecution. "No." "Did you notice injuries to his calves or arm?" "No, I did not see any injuries. Obviously there was blood on his shorts and on his shirt but we took both of them to be tested."

Brnovich asked if there were injuries to his hands. On the bottom of his right palm, there was a cut mark. She showed the detective pictures of the cut hand and asked if there were injuries to his left hand. "No. There was a slight injury to the left side of his left-hand middle finger, in the knuckle area."

Brnovich asked D'Aguanno if he attended the autopsy of Vina Bartlett and he explained to the jury that he had. Asked if the police take pictures during autopsies, he told the court they did and six of the autopsy photos were scrutinized in the courtroom.

"After you attended the autopsy, did you interview Tracy at the hospital?" D'Aguanno explained he did—it was after my surgery. He spoke to me for half an hour. He explained how our discussion was surrounding my asking him why the police didn't come in to help me sooner. I had been concerned about bonds and charges against Frank.

Susan Brnovich wanted the jury to know if Detective D'Aguanno went to the clinic where I'd worked to get the security video. He said he had. She asked if he requested a blood sample from the deceased victim, Vina Bartlett, and from me. "Yes. They also cut carpet from the home and took blood samples from the blinds in the downstairs room."

Canby did the cross-examination. He asked, "Isn't it true Vina had a red hair clip in her hair the day of the autopsy?" Was Frank's lawyer trying to insinuate there wasn't a struggle because my mother still had a clip in her hair?

Canby said, "You wrote 'removed hair clip'." D'Aguanno said "I don't know. The hair clip was in the bag. All I know is that how I wrote it was "removed from the victim." Unemotionally, they showed him more pictures of my mother during the autopsy. I couldn't watch the screen and I had to turn my head. I heard my grandmother crying behind me in the spectator seats. A year still wasn't enough time to be able to look at these pictures without feeling the pain.

One picture had my mother lying out in front of the residence, then a picture on the backboard the SWAT team used. Canby said, "Doesn't it appear her hair is tied back in the picture?" D'Aguanno said, "I see a red hair clip on her head in the picture but I don't

Chapter Twelve | Court Injustice

know how her hair is tied back." So they argued about her hair for a while.

Mr. Canby asked D'Aguanno, "Do you remember telling the Grand Jury there were no choke marks on Tracy's neck?" "I don't remember," D'Aguanno said. Canby questioned D'Aguanno longer, I thought, simply trying to discredit him.

The state's prosecution, Susan Brnovich, asked Detective D'Aguanno if the knife marks on the hands of the defendant could be made from the knife sliding down his hand while he was using it. He was sure, "Yes, Ma'am.

She had no more questions, so they released him and swore in Detective Laird. He was an assigned scene investigator for the location. They talked about the photos of my mother in the garage across the street and what pictures they have to take in a crime scene. Laird painted verbal pictures of blood trails from the front door going eastbound across the street, slightly north, and into a garage. Susan showed pictures of my mother's handprint on the garage wall. That picture cries volumes about the suffering my mother felt as she died. He explained that the handprint appeared as if someone leaned against the wall, the blood ran down the wall to the floor, and the blood pool is where the victim laid. The second trail of blood was caused by the officers taking her body on the gurney to the street corner.

Susan asked what Laird first did on arrival at the scene and he said he took mental pictures to organize it in his mind, and then his evidence technicians took actual photos.

Brnovich asked him if he saw anything unusual when he first walked into the crime scene. He said he saw bloody footprints. They asked about the blood on the stair wall. He described how blood was on the railing, the wall, and in footprints. She showed him pictures of the sewing kit in the bedroom. In the box was the broken serrated knife. The handle lying parallel above the blade.

They asked if the knife was broken when he found it and he said yes. Detective Laird said he took it as evidence. He explained what it looked like. He said it was a black-handled knife, broken at the handle. "It's serrated and blood stained along the blade." Then they talked about the pictures of the blood soaked clothing at the end of the bed; my uniform from the clinic. Susan asked if the clothes would have been cut off of me. "Yes."

Detective Laird's report written on August 1, 2001 read in part:

> "During walk-through of the first floor of the apartment, we discovered an extremely large amount of blood and bloody feet prints throughout the apartment. The initial entryway, dining room and kitchen had a linoleum tile floor. This floor contained a large number of bloody bare feet prints. The remainder of the downstairs area, the living room, the stairwell, the bedroom, the bathroom and the walk-in closet were all carpeted floor. These carpeted floors were also covered with bloody feet prints, blood trails and at least two large pools of blood.
>
> We began an initial walk through of the second floor area. As we climbed the stairs, we noticed a number of bloody feet prints and blood smears on the floor and walls.
>
> Immediately to your right is the doorway into what is apparently a child's bedroom. This bedroom had an extremely large amount of toys and stuffed animals. This bedroom also had a number of bloody footprints and blood smears on the walls in various locations."

Laird's report described other areas upstairs and concluded with, "The second floor, as with the bottom floor contained a large amount of blood pools, blood trails and bloody feet prints."

Chapter Twelve | Court Injustice

After Detective Laird's testimony, Chief Medical Examiner, Dr. Keen, was sworn in. He was asked how many autopsies he'd performed. He said his ten thousandth autopsy had been the previous year. He explained his job, its responsibilities, and what it entailed. He confirmed he did the autopsy on my mother. He explained, "Vina had a stab wound on the left of her neck about the head of the clavicle and the muscle that runs from the clavicle to the back of the ear. It's approximately an inch and a half to the left of the midline. The shape of the wound was V-shaped, consistent with a single cutting edge object like a knife. The wound was seven-eighths to an inch long, and it penetrated backwards and downward for a distance of approximately two and three-quarter inches and it went through the soft tissues of the neck and terminated in where the aortic arch comes off the heart and then goes down to supply the main vascular supplied to the body. Between that artery that would then come off of the ear and go up to neck, the carotid, and the artery that would come off the ear, go to the left arm, right between those two arteries is approximately a half-inch slice in the aorta. From that slice in the aorta there was bleeding into the sack around the heart and bleeding into the chest. And that, essentially, is the wound —it is a wound which is essentially lethal and fatal."

Brnovich asked Dr. Keen to talk about the knife and how it appeared, the discolorations, and the broken handle.

She asked, "Now, I believe you already indicated that that wound is fatal?" Keen answered, "That was a fatal wound."

Brnovich asked Dr. Keene several questions about my mother's other injuries. Which ones had already existed, like superficial bruises, and which ones were results of the attack.

"You also mentioned some injuries to her fingertips?"

"Yes, of the left hand."

"I will look for that photograph. But how were those described and on what fingers?"

"The right index finger has a superficial abrasion the base of the nail bed, and on the left ring finger there is a superficial incised wound approximately a quarter inch long. But these — and I — when I was reviewing photos, of these, these are superficial slightly angled wounds that are probably no deeper than about a 16th on an inch. And they happened to be angled so the bleeding is actually under one edge of the wound and not under the other."

My mother was right-handed. These wounds could be nothing other than defensive injuries received when she held up her hands to protect her face. They could not have been, as the defense claimed, self injuries incurred while holding a knife.

Thursday, August 8th, 2002 (which happened to be Frank's birthday) was the last day of the trial. Just another day it seemed as I awoke to the sounds of my clock radio. I showered and put on my makeup and dressed out in my businesswoman-like attire. Yet, as I drove through traffic, my hands would not stop shaking. All I could remember was how this monster disguised as one of us humans murdered my mom and tried to kill me. So I drove on—I could not wait till I saw the look on his face when he was found guilty on all counts.

Once at the court building, all "remnants of just another day" went out the window. I found my seat as soon as possible. Once in the courtroom, everything slowed down. I could hear murmurs and whispers and every now and then some "suit" would stop and give his or her condolences.

Then finally everyone was seated. *He* was in the room! He glared at me.

The attorneys and the judge discussed allowing the jury to see the videotaped interview between a detective and Frank on the night of the attack. The tape was viewed by the jury, but nothing was noted in the court transcripts because they considered the tape itself to be its own best evidence.

They agreed that there was no cross-examination or rebuttal necessary. With the jury, they reviewed final instructions, burden of proof, evidence, and presumption of innocence for quite some time. Then we began closing arguments. Eighteen pages worth of transcripts explaining instructions.

Susan Brnovich spoke next. Her closing arguments covered nineteen pages of transcript.

> **MS. BRNOVICH:** "Thank you, Your Honor, and thank you, ladies and gentlemen, for your attention throughout the case and throughout the interruptions in this case. As most of the things that I'm going to have up, there are photographs that have been admitted, so if it gets distracting to look at the pictures and listen, I'd rather have you looking at me.
>
> These are just to sort of point out where it is that I think the important evidence is. But everything you see, you will have back in the deliberation room with you. The defendant's statement "She is cheating on me." That tells you what this is all about. It comes up several times. And Tracy Stombres had her face mutilated by the defendant, because he didn't want her to be attractive anymore. He didn't want her attracting the attention of other men, like Cory Klander. His obsession with this Cory Klander issue started earlier that day when he confronted Cory. He didn't happen to just show up on the one day that Cory is going to come over. And he talks to Cory Klander. It's just a simple conversation in the parking lot. Its 45 minutes. He drives him around, gets him something to eat, something to drink. Chats with him. Tries to fish with him, you know, she is attractive, she is good looking. I would understand why you did it. And although he says he came home

from work because he is sick, he spends all this time with Mr. Klander. And then instead of waiting for his wife to come home, he has to go confront her now, and he goes to her work place around noon and he confronts her there at work. But of course she is at work, so not a whole lot can take place, so he goes home. And what do you think he is thinking about for the four hours before Tracy gets home? Cory Klander. And when he gets home or when Tracy gets home, they start talking. And Cory calls, which is the whole center of all of this. And it sets him off again and they start arguing. And this is where the argument starts in their bedroom. They start arguing, Tracy takes off her shoes. He pushes her, chokes her, she slaps him. I'm sure she does. He's calling her a bitch, telling her — he is confronting her about sleeping with another man. Then she goes out. He follows her. And they are in that area that is like the dinette area, but there is no dining room table, so it's essentially an open room. But it's right by the stairs. And her mom can hear the screaming going on downstairs. So her mom comes down to make sure that everything is okay. And the defendant is not going to put up with any crap from his wife or his mother-in-law. He goes into the kitchen. And he has the information about where the knife comes from. He pulls two women into the kitchen. You will see from the pictures — I mean, it's not like he is pulling them very far. It's like five feet. Pulls them into the kitchen to get the knife. They wrestle. I mean, these women aren't going to want to get cut with the knife. The struggle moves out of the kitchen. Things get knocked over. Out in the living room Vina realizes she is bleeding, stands there, and says, "I'm bleeding." Her blood is in the living room, and she leaves. Once she realizes she is bleeding and leaves, that's it. You heard from Dr. Keen that she is not going to make it much longer than it takes to walk across the street. So she is out of the picture. And Tracy — this is most likely from Vina walking out in her bare feet: You will see the pictures of Vina, and she is covered with blood. And she has got bare feet. She is in a shirt and shorts from just hanging out at her house. She makes it across the street, almost to the door. And you can see where she put her hand up to the wall to lean, and just died. And this is where the officers who testified told you they found her. And they didn't even see her right away. And Vina is taken off a back board, but the paramedics said it's so obvious she is dead; all they do is cover her up. So she makes it outside of the house, and Tracy is not so lucky. She is pulled into her bedroom, and the defendant starts going off on her. He is hitting her. He is kicking her. He is cutting her. There is blood on the bed. There is blood on the floor. There is blood on the blinds. There is blood everywhere. There is hair on the bed and on the floor. It' either being pulled out or cut. This is where Tracy told you that she is essentially huddled on the floor trying to protect her face and protecting her throat from the defendant. Tracy's blood. This is her hair on the carpet. At some point defendant decides to take it upstairs, and he pulls her upstairs. You can see her handprint on the stairwell where she grabs on for support. And at this point how much struggling do you think Tracy is going to be able to give? She has been kicked, punched, cut. She is losing blood, and she is probably scared. And she's taken up and thrown on the floor in her mother's room. Now, while they are up there — you know, and this is taking a while. You see the number of cuts Tracy has. That doesn't come from a single swipe at Tracy's face. It takes them time. So they get upstairs and the defendant calls her grandmother, Lillian Calderon that you heard from. And says — doesn't tell her what happened. Says, 'Call my mom. I need to talk to my mom.' So Lillian calls his mother. His mother calls him back and he says, "I cut Tracy." And, you know, his mom asked, you know, if she is okay. And he gets off the phone with her and doesn't call 911. I mean, this whole time he is not calling 911. He doesn't call Lillian back and tell her to call 911. His mother calls Lillian back and says, 'Call the police. I don't really know what is going on, but Tracy has been cut.' So Lillian thankfully calls 911. And while he is up there, he puts the knife away in a sewing box where it's found. And you'll have it so you can take a look at it. So the 911 call — well, Officer Ray told us 5:15 was his dispatch, so I put it up there 5:14, because essentially the 911 call would have come out before he is dispatched. But there is, you know, a time frame of 45 minutes, give or take, 45 minutes, a half hour between the time Tracy comes home and 911 is called. Then there is an hour and 20 minutes before the defendant gives up. During that time frame, Officer Ray makes phone calls to him. Gets him on the phone. This is what Frank did. What does he say? 'She has been cheating on me.' That is what is in his head at that time. That's what he is thinking about. Not help me. Not help my wife. Not help my mother-in-law. Me, me, me, me. She is cheating on me. And then still in the

> aggressive mode he says, 'I don't want to shoot a cop. I better not see one.' Officer Ray arrives at the house. Actually, physically arrives at the house. Continues his conversations trying to keep the defendant on the phone, tells the defendant, once by finding Vina and see her laying there in the garage, he tries to get the defendant to come out, so they can get her length photo of him. But his shorts — most of the blood is on the inside of the legs, like he was straddling Tracy. It's not like on the outside here, so just take a look at that, and ask, why is the blood in that portion of his shorts? Tracy goes to the hospital and goes almost directly into surgery. Once they have got her on some blood. And Tracy is not able to be interviewed, photographed until the next day. And she is in the hospital on pain medication, but she tells Detective D'Aguanno what she can remember."

While all nineteen pages of closing arguments are important, these were the first six pages. Susan's goal was to remind the jury of what Frank did – and what he failed to do.

John Canby took a different angle. He appealed to the jury's sense of self-esteem and made them feel sorry for him, and for Frank.

> **CANBY:** "Thank you, Your Honor. Counsel, ladies and gentlemen of the jury, first thing I would like to do is thank you for your service. I don't know if you noticed that in jury selection that anybody who stood up and said I can't be fair was pretty much gone pretty quickly. Obviously, if any of you had really wanted to get out of jury service bad enough, you heard the magic words, and you could have said that. We selected you because we felt you would be

fair. And I have noticed throughout the case that you have been paying close attention, taking notes, asking good questions. And on behalf of my client, I would like to thank you for your service in this case and your attention. I also want to talk a little bit about the way this closing argument works. Now, the State goes first, the second — defense goes second, and the State goes again. And so that puts the defense at a slight disadvantage. Now, the reason, we're also told, for that order of presentation is that the State has the burden of proof, so they get to go twice. Now, I never understood that, because it seems to me if they have the burden of proof and we get the benefit of the doubt, that we ought to get to go twice, but that's not the rule, so since I'm only going to go once, one thing I ask you to do is remember that if something is said after I sit down that may not accurately reflect your memory of something that I might have been able to retort, think about what I might have said, because I don't get a chance to stand back up. And obviously the State has the opportunity to say things that won't be rebutted, but I trust your memory is sufficient to rebut things that are not accurate that you are told.

And that brings up another point. The things that the lawyers say in argument are not evidence. So just because we stand up and say something happened in this trial, or somebody said something, that doesn't make it so. You look at your notes. You use your collective memory. You decide what happened in this trial, not me, and not Ms. Brnovich. One thing that has become clear in this case is there are some things that will be disputed and there are some things that are and really you are going to be called

Chapter Twelve | Court Injustice

upon to resolve the issues that are in dispute in this case. There is no question that there was some kind of altercation that day. There is also no question that it at least in the beginning began around a discussion involving Cory Klander. Nobody is disputing that. And it's also clear that as a result of that altercation, that Vina Bartlett died and that Tracy Stombres ended up with several cuts and bruises, but the key issues in this case, even with those things not being disputed, are yet to be decided. Did Frank cause these injuries? If he didn't cause the injury, particularly with respect to Vina, then he is not guilty. One thing you need to see — I don't know if you noticed when the second degree murder was up there, but each one of the three ways to commit second degree murder included element. Causing the death of another. So if he didn't cause the death of Vina, then he is not guilty. If he did cause the death of Vina, then the issue becomes, was he justified under the law in doing so. Because that's what self defense and crime prevention are. They are justification statutes that make what others liable look like conduct justified under the law. And if justification applies, the defendant is not guilty. Now, on page five of your instructions, there is a reasonable doubt instruction that the judge read to you. And I know you have taken a look at that as the judge talked, but one of the things I want to point out is what it really comes down to. You know, reasonable doubt is a hard thing to define. You heard it all your life, probably, if you have been exposed to the justice system, but I don't know if it's like the Supreme Court used to say, but we know it when we see it, but reasonable doubt, I think it's something like that. I think you know when you see it and when it's in front of you, but from our point of those parts of reasonable doubt is that if you think there is a real possibility that an element is not established, then the person should be found not guilty of the charge which contains that element, because the burden of proof applies to each element, not just the crime in general, but each element of the crime. Now, there is a bunch of — as the instructions said, we have different burdens in law. And the lowest burden of proof or the lowest standard that has to be met — see if I can make this work — is reasonable suspicion. Okay. One of the reasons I like using this is because the State's using it and I don't want to be left behind in the technology. (He's referring to a LCD projector for Power Point). And if I have a little trouble with it, please bear with me, because I'm used to overhead projector presentations, but I'm going to try this anyway. But getting back to reasonable — this is going to be difficult. I get going too fast, so I hope the court reporter can bear with me, because I have a lot to say and I really want to say it. But reasonable suspicion is that level of suspicion that a police officer would need to pull you over for, say, a traffic offense. Not enough to charge you with the crime, but enough to pull you over, and maybe what is called an investigative stop to see why it is that, you know, your light was out or your taillight isn't working. The next level is probable cause. Probable cause is what it takes to arrest somebody. It's not proof beyond a reasonable doubt and it's not enough to assume anybody is guilty. But it's enough to start a case with an arrest.

Chapter Twelve | Court Injustice

Preponderance of the evidence. That's the burden of proof in a civil case. When money is at stake. Okay. One side. That really means it's more likely to be than not, so if in a civil case, if you are suing for money, really all you have to do is weigh the scales over to one side and make it more probable than not.

Now, there is another level that is in between preponderance of the evidence and beyond a reasonable doubt, and that's clear and convincing evidence. In some civil matters or for some matters, for instance, when the State is trying to say they think you are not taking care of your child and they want to put the child in protective custody or CPS custody, what is required in those kinds of cases is clear and convincing evidence. But the highest level of proof in the legal system is that which is applied to a criminal trial, once again beyond a reasonable doubt. There is really only one level of proof above that, and that's absolute certainty. But you know from the jury selection process that we pick people who don't know anything about this case, people who weren't there, so, you know, the State is not required to prove somebody guilty to an absolute certainty, but the point I'm trying to make here is this is a very high level of proof. It's a level of proof that protects each and every one of you if you were to be accused of something by the Government. You have that protection and everybody has that protection, including Mr. Gomez. I have mentioned that — before I get to the justification statutes, really the way it makes sense to go about looking at the crimes with which my client is charged is first of all, did the State prove the elements of the crime beyond a reasonable doubt? And if they didn't, you don't need to look to justification to see if the conduct was justified. It's just they haven't met the level of proof required, and Mr. Gomez should be found not guilty. As I indicated with the second degree murder charge to Vina Bartlett, each one of those ways of committing that crime requires that Mr. Gomez caused the death of Vina Bartlett. And given what we have heard, you know, really in some ways depends who you believe. Certainly if Frank got the knife first and stabbed Vina with it, then he caused her death.

But if the injury occurred while people were fighting over the knife, for instance, when the knife was released or when you are trying to fight with somebody and that was — the resistance is gone or you are trying to pull back and maybe you come into yourself, that if the injury occurred in that way, and the State has to prove beyond a reasonable doubt that it didn't, so if there is a real possibility given what you heard that that's the way it occurred, then he is not guilty of second degree murder, because there is lack of causation. But if you think that the knife was purposely put in Vina, that doesn't end the analysis. You are still going to have to look at whether that act was justified under either the crime prevention or self defense statutes."

In the twenty-three total pages of transcripts, these are Canby's first six, but already, he craftily uses tactics to make Frank look innocent.

Susan Brnovich concluded her several page rebuttal with:
"As I mentioned, the justification statutes are

something that you really don't get to unless you believe the defendant's story. If you believe that Vina got the knife first, then you have to ask whether or not the defendant acted reasonably. He is the one starting the fight with his wife. Tracy's mom comes downstairs to intervene. If you believe his story, then she goes to get the knife. He is on his out anyway, according to what he said, so he doesn't leave, although he knows it's now getting heated. So is that reasonable? Then he gets attacked, but he grabs her hand and he is able to get the knife away within 10 to 11 seconds, and the threat is gone. And at that point there are two unarmed women and he has got the knife. And if you believe his story, then at that point he would have had to have stabbed Vina in self defense and then gone after Tracy, because nothing happened before he got the knife. I mean, he didn't get cut or anything, so he grabs her wrist, takes the knife away, and then goes after both of them. None of these are reasonable under the self defense statute. The force used or threatened to be used by the defendant may not be greater than what is reasonably necessary to repel the danger. Slicing up Tracy's face that many times is not reasonable to repel any danger from Tracy. The right to use or threaten to use deadly physical force in self defense ends when the apparent danger ends. And when he takes the knife away, there is no longer a deadly threat to him, if you believe his story. In light of what we know about the injuries to Tracy and the injury to Vina, we know that this did not occur in a fight for his life. The injuries would have been much more random, not concentrated. And that stab wound to Vina just wouldn't have happened in a fight over the knife. If he is — first of all, if it appears the way he said it did, the knife is coming at him, not at Vina. If he gets the knife and he is punching at Tracy, even if somehow he swings back and hits Vina, again, it's going in a different direction. It is not going straight down like as if he is standing above her and plunging it in or standing next to her and plunging it in. The physical evidence of the injuries alone tells you that this didn't occur in a fight, and that the defendant was the aggressor. We know why he was the aggressor. Unfortunately, Vina got in the middle of it and got the worst of it. But the defendant is not the victim here. And I'd ask that you hold him accountable. Thank you."

After that, the judge released the entire courtroom for lunch. He reminded the jury not to speak about the trial until after lunch. At that time, when all twelve had reconvened, they would be sequestered to begin deliberations.

The jury deliberated from 12:49 p.m. to 3:47 p.m. Three hours. Only three. Every minute they were gone caused me anxiety, but the speed in which they returned troubled me. I wondered, does a short deliberation mean their minds were already made up? Who would they favor? I watched them come in to take their seats, apprehension eating its way through my stomach. Finally the jury was back with the verdict after a short, nasty trial. I couldn't wait to hear it.

THE COURT: "Good afternoon, members of the jury. You are welcome to have a seat. The record shows you are present. We have the attorneys on both sides, Mr. Gomez, the case agent, court reporter and staff also present. This question is directed to your foreperson. Has the jury reached a verdict?"

Chapter Twelve | Court Injustice

THE FOREPERSON: "Yes, we have, Your Honor."

THE COURT: "Okay. Thank you. If you'll please hand the verdict forms to the bailiff, she'll bring them to me.

Okay. The clerk will please read and record the verdicts."

THE CLERK: "We, the Jury, Duly empanelled and sworn in the above—entitled action upon our oaths, do find the defendant, Frank Gomez as to Count 1, second degree murder of Vina Marie Bartlett: Not guilty. Signed foreperson.

We, the Jury, duly empanelled and sworn in the above—entitled action upon our oaths, do find the defendant, Frank Gomez as to the lesser included offense in Count 1, Manslaughter by sudden quarrel or heat of passion (Vina Marie Bartlett): Not guilty. Signed foreperson.

We, the Jury, duly empanelled and sworn in the above—entitled action upon our oaths, do find the defendant, Frank Gomez as to Count 2, attempted first degree murder (Tracy Ann Stombres): Not guilty. Signed foreperson.

We, the Jury, duly empanelled and sworn in the above-entitled action upon our oaths, do find the defendant, Frank Gomez in the alternative as to Count 2, aggravated assault (Tracy Ann Stombres): Guilty.

We, the Jury, further find the offense to be a dangerous offense: True. Signed foreperson.

We, the Jury, duly empanelled and sworn in the above-entitled action upon our oaths, do find the defendant, Frank Gomez as to Count 3, kidnapping (Tracy Ann Stombres): Guilty.

We, the Jury, further find the offense to be a dangerous offense: True. Signed foreperson.

We, the Jury, duly empanelled and sworn in the above-entitled action upon our oaths, do find the defendant, Frank Gomez as to Count 4, kidnapping (Vina Marie Bartlett): Not guilty. Signed foreperson.

Not guilty! What?! How was this possible? This monster took the life out of my precious mother! This pig disfigured me and found pleasure in torturing me till he thought I was dead. This could not be!

I was sick, disoriented, and dizzy. I felt like vomiting. Then rage almost overcame me and I felt like running at him and smacking him across the face! But no, I can't. So as the hush falls over the crowd, I drown in surreal-ness. Other verdicts get read off that I can barely hear or understand. I'm dumfounded. My mom just got murdered all over again. My scars hurt, my heart hurt, and my faith in the justice system was shattered!

They didn't even find him guilty of attempted murder on me? What the …? How was this possible? Finally, I stared at every one of the jurors with tears in my eyes and face pleading to stand up and change their minds. **Please! Help! Please!** Someone? God? *Anybody!* He's getting away with *murder!* Yes, he got away with murder. Just like he said he would.

I often think jurors forget just how many people are affected by their decisions. I had an entire family that was traumatized, each in his or her own way. My grandmother, the mother of a murdered daughter, wrote this about her reaction:

Chapter Twelve | Court Injustice

As if it wasn't enough to lose my daughter and very close to losing my granddaughter, I thought that we would get a break from the judicial system. When the verdict was read, saying "Not Guilty" on my daughter's murder and only giving him 12 years for the torture, beating and stabbing he did to my granddaughter, I felt as if I had been punched in my stomach. I lost my breath, I went numb. I wanted to get up and scream or run out of the court room screaming. To this day I am still *very depressed!* As for the judicial system and the jurors; they made us the victims twice. What came to my mind was *here we go again. We have another repetition of the O.J. Simpson trail. A murderer getting away with murder.* I am always told that time heals all wounds, but I am having a hard time believing that. Maybe one of these days the judicial system will give the victims of abuse a break and really punish the abusers and give them what they really deserve.

On September 18, 2002, Susan Brnovich, on behalf of Maricopa County Attorney, Richard Romley, wrote an eight page sentencing memorandum to the judge. It began:

> The State hereby submits the attached sentencing memorandum in support of its recommendation that the defendant be sentenced to the aggravated terms of 15 years on Count 2, Aggravated Assault, and 21 years on Count 3, Kidnapping.

The last page concluded:

> The defendant's criminal history and past acts of violence demonstrate that the defendant is very likely

to re-offend. He should be kept off the streets for as long as possible solely because of that information. However, we also have the aggravating factors of the harm to Lillian, Tracy and Alex. Tracy will eventually finish her physical rehabilitation. She will live forever with physical and emotional scars as well as the hepatitis that threatens her life. Alex will hopefully be able to overcome his fears through counseling. Alex will never regain the time that he has lived in fear instead of enjoying as a child. Based on all of the information provided, the State requests that you sentence the defendant to the maximum sentences allowed under the law.

I looked at this as good news. Frank would be in prison for fifteen years. In that time, I could rebuild me life and my children would reach legal adulthood. He'd be out of their lives.

September 20, 2002 - sentencing day. The judge said he'd received letters from my family members, which he'd read to the court. Four people got to speak about what they wanted in terms of sentencing. The first up was Scott Bruce, my mother's boyfriend. He began to talk about how my mother was quite a person and he felt it wasn't brought out enough. The judge told him that "Mr. Gomez was not found guilty of Vina Bartlett's death and couldn't be held accountable for it." The judge said, in other words, the law found self-defense under the law. The jury found that "Mr. Gomez did not commit a crime against Vina Bartlett, and I'm not going to allow you to talk about Vina Bartlett. She no longer is a victim in this case." So Scott asked if he could talk about her daughter. He said, "This has affected her life and her kids' lives. I think he had a choice he could have made and walked away from that. I mean she is scared for her life and now she is without a mother and that's all I have to say."

Chapter Twelve | Court Injustice

My aunt, Liz Jolly, went on the stand. She spoke articulately, "Today you will have the power and discretion to sentence Frank Gomez to incarceration for his crimes. During trial, several of his previous violent contacts could not be brought before the jury. He has a history of domestic violence upon Tracy and at least one former girlfriend. During an argument with Tracy he once hit her hard enough to cause her to fall and break her leg. He cannot control his actions, unless he uses force to solve his problems". Liz went on to talk about Chelsea calling her house on several occasions when she was scared and that Chelsea witnessed acts of violence that no child should have to see.

A jury found Frank Gomez innocent of Vina's death. And as irrational as we find that to be, we must accept that verdict and go on with our lives. However he could have stopped his attack on his wife at any time. Instead he chose to air out his jealous rage on her regardless, beating and stabbing her relentlessly, all in the presence of his son, Alex. This child will carry these memories with him all his life. What kind of remorse or feelings does he have? He calls Lillian's house from jail collect and also has sent mail to Alex at her address. What kind of person does this? One who apparently doesn't believe he did anything wrong. One who has no concern for anyone other than himself. He continues to hurt others, he has no conscious. Your honor, you have the power to see that Frank Gomez receives a punishment he deserves and is held accountable for his actions. It would be too much to expect that we live free in a non-violent world. But the laws of our country are the only resource we have to punish those who violate the laws that protect the criminals also. Judges such as yourself are the ones we have to rely upon to carry out not only the law but to carry out justice for the families and all victims who must continue to live each day with the senseless violence these criminals commit."

She went on to urge the judge to give Frank a harsh, but appropriate, sentence. Then said, "Perhaps then he'll have a long time to reflect on how much pain he caused everyone including his son Alex, and Chelsea, his young stepdaughter and perhaps he will also find the courage to accept his punishment and realize that it is he who has put himself in his situation and not blame anyone else for his actions."

My friend, Valerie, spoke next. "I have seen the bruising on Tracy's body and it seemed towards the end it escalated to the point to where he wanted to take her life and to the point to where she couldn't get away from him and she felt defeated. I have seen her move out lots of times. She can't have a balanced life. She can't build a future for herself. Frank tears it all apart and she has to start over again."

Valerie told the judge that she wanted to hire a private investigator to protect me but couldn't afford it. "The police were never there on time to help her. Frank has been doing this for a long time." She asked that "Frank get the maximum sentence for Tracy's protection so Tracy could go on with her life and give her children the type of life they deserved."

These words of support from family and friends meant the world to me. At the end, I finally got my turn to speak. And it was my first chance to speak uncensored. The following is directly from the court transcripts that day:

> **MS. STOMBRES:** "I'd like to start off with saying some things I was not able to say in court, like he has been in prison twice before. He has beaten me for five years. He almost killed me in Vegas. He almost killed me in Mexico. He has beaten his ex-girlfriend. He pulled a knife on her chest. He had all these things I could not say during trial which I don't understand why."
>
> **THE COURT:** "Well, the State's lawyer can tell you why. There are rules of evidence so juries don't decide cases on passion, but decide it strictly on the facts derived on the evidence, so –"

Chapter Twelve | Court Injustice

MS. STOMBRES: "So that makes the jurors think this is some perfect, innocent guy who had never been in trouble before?"

THE COURT: "I'm not here to argue with you. And know you are not a lawyer. So we trust the lawyers that the cases follow the rules of evidence, so the procedure is as fair as possible a procedure whether the outcome from the parties is a different story."

MS. BRNOVICH: "Judge, just so you know, we have talked about this stuff. She knows why legally, but this is her opportunity to tell you her frustrations, how this has affected her."

MS. STOMBRES: "And also, I was not able to use her as a witness when –"

THE COURT: "You are not able to use?"

MS. STOMBRES: "His ex-girlfriend as a witness when he had used a knife on her. I couldn't use her as a witness. Frank has hurt a lot of us. He writes my grandma all the time. He calls her collect. He says he is going to be out in five years to get my son, so obviously he already assumed he is only going to do five years. Obviously, his lawyer told him or somebody has told him, because when he came in here for trial, he knew he was going to get out of this. I don't know if his lawyer told him something or what. When he wrote my girlfriend, he said he'd be out in five years and to get my son. So I don't understand what makes him think he is going to get out in five years. But that's another thing that I want to bring up, too, that he wrote my grandmother and said — and also my grandmother is on medication for depression. My son is on medication. My daughter is on medication, and I'm on medication. We have been diagnosed with post traumatic stress disorder. I have nightmares every night. My son is mentally disturbed. He has severe post traumatic stress disorder. I have Hepatitis C through him using a knife on my mother and then using the knife on me. My blood got infected, because of her blood. I didn't have Hepatitis C when I was in the hospital. When I got out, I got real sick and got diagnosed with Hepatitis C. Now I'm infected. I had a liver biopsy done last week, two chunks of my liver taken out. My liver is really bad. It's already getting totally sick. I have to start injections next week. I will be giving myself injections in the leg four times a week for a year. And I'm hoping it will cure it or I will be dead with my mother too. I'm not going to be able to watch my kids grow if I die from this Hepatitis C. It's a fatal disease that he knew my mother had.

And also, I wanted to let you know that he endangered my son and there was no kind of charge for child endangerment. He let my son see me get stabbed. Blood everywhere. My son saw everything. My son stabs toys up. My son constantly stabs his trucks, his cars, because he'd seen him doing it. And he has a whole different way of thinking compared to other kids. What else. I'm going to be sick in bed whole year. I'm not going to be able to work. I'm not going to be able to take care of my kids, because of the Hepatitis C. Like I told you, he killed me almost three others times in Vegas. I had to jump out of a three-story building almost because of him. I didn't know if I could jump out of the building to get away from him. He took me to Mexico, left me on the beach out there, beat me almost to death on the sand, and almost raped me there. He always told me he would get away with anything. He told my grandparents he would get away with anything. He told me he could always get away with murder. He told me he would get away with murder and obviously he was right about that. And I would just hope that you give him the maximum sentence. The highest maximum sentence there is. If he gets out soon, he'll just finish me off. There is no doubt about it. And he'll probably get his son and end up hurting him. And I would like to watch my kids grow up if I could, if I don't die before that with Hepatitis C. Thank you."

After court was finally over, the kids and I tried to get our lives on track and forget. I knew it was time to take care of the hepatitis situation. I had decided to wait till after trial. So, as soon as the trial was over, I started treatment. The doctor said I'd be in the injections about a year and to be prepared to be in bed a lot and to get help with my children. I started the treatment. I had to inject my stomach and legs. It would make me sick. I lost a lot of weight and lost my hair. It can cause psychosis, suicidal thoughts, anorexia, and depression. I stayed in the house a lot and tried to be with my kids as much as I could while feeling so sick. Before I started the injections, I sat down with my children and explained what we were going to have to go through and about the disease. I went to support groups. After about six months of injections, the doctor said there was no sign of the Hepatitis C any longer but he wanted me to stay on treatment for the whole year just in case it came back. After a year, there was still no sign. I told him I was trying to exercise a lot and I had a lot of natural remedies for liver health. I drank lots of water and he said I probably got rid of it because we knew the day I got it and we started treatment as soon as possible.

A few weeks after the verdict, on September 18, 2002, Susan Brnovich, on behalf of Maricopa County Attorney Richard Romley, had given an eight-page memo to the Superior Court Judge Louis Araneta, asking that Frank receive "the maximum sentences allowed under the law." She said the State's "recommendation that the defendant be sentenced to the aggravated terms of 15 years on Count 2, Aggravated Assault, and 21 years on Count 3, Kidnapping. Count 2 carries a presumptive sentence of 7.5 years; a minimum sentence of 5 years, and the maximum is 15 years. Count 3 carries a presumptive sentence of 10.5 years; a minimum sentence of 7 years, and the maximum is 21 years."

Frank received nine and a half years for the assault, and twelve for kidnapping. The Judge decided he could run his sentences concurrently, not consecutively, and he would only have to serve time for the higher of the two sentences. In the end, Frank was sentenced to twelve years and credited for time already served. Twelve years for all of it. Everything.

SERRATED

News Release
Stombres v. ——— Civil Trial Scheduled

In a case reminiscent of the O.J. Simpson trials, a Phoenix woman is suing her ex husband for killing her mother during a domestic violence assault.

In an August 1, 2001 act of domestic violence, ——— used a kitchen knife and scissors to inflict multiple lacerations to the face and body of his estranged wife Tracy Stombres. Their two year old son witnessed the malaise. Tracy's mother, Vina Bartlett of Phoenix, was also present and while trying to save Tracy's life, suffered a stab wound to her own neck and fled the house to get help from neighbors. When Phoenix police arrived, ——— told the police he had a gun. During the police hostage standoff, ——— refused to release their son, or allow Tracy to receive medical attention. Just prior to the standoff ending with ——— arrest, police discovered Vina Bartlett's body in a neighbor's garage. She had bled to death. Stombres survived the ordeal but required extensive reconstructive surgery, including the surgical reattachment of her nose.

During the week long criminal trial, ——— claimed that he was a victim of domestic violence acting in self defense, and that Stombres' mother must have been accidentally stabbed in the neck during a struggle for the knife. On August 8, 2002, ——— was criminally convicted of aggravated assault and kidnapping of Tracy Stombres. However, the Maricopa County jury acquitted ——— of the 1st degree murder charge of Vina Bartlett. ——— was sentenced to twelve years in prison, with probability that he will be released after serving nine years.

Believing that she witnessed her mother's murder but that criminal justice was not served, Tracy Stombres turned to the civil justice system. On July 29, 2003, Stombres filed a civil law suit against ——— for her injuries from the aggravated assault, as well as for the wrongful death of her mother.

Stombres is represented by Kent Phelps, senior litigation attorney of the Never Again Foundation, a non profit charity that began in Arizona in 2001. The Foundation provides free civil legal representation to women, children, and elders who have been physically or sexually abused, and files lawsuits directly against the abusers. The goal is to help provide hope, justice, and healing to crime victims by holding criminals accountable through the civil justice system, while simultaneously sending strong messages of prevention and legal awareness throughout society. The foundation has obtained more than $50 million in judgments for crime victims in Arizona during the past four years. 100% of all judgments collected are given to help the victims rebuild their lives.

The trial is scheduled to begin April 4, 2005, and is expected to last four days. The case (#CV 2003-———) will be presided over by Judge ——— of the Maricopa County Superior Court, Southeast Judicial complex in Mesa, Arizona. The not guilty verdict of the underlying criminal case gained national attention and was aired on the Montel Williams program of July 24, 2003. For more information, contact Keith Perkins, the Founding Attorney & Executive Director of the Never Again Foundation at (480) 539-9111, or by e-mail at keith@neveragainfoundation.org.

Thirteen

NEVER AGAIN

The Arizona Coalition Against Domestic Violence told me about a start-up non-profit law firm that wanted to do civil suits for victims of domestic violence, The Never Again Foundation. Their lawyers would provide free legal representation for victims of domestic violence, sexual assault, or elder abuse in civil lawsuits directly against the abusers.

All of the money collected is given to victims to help rebuild their lives. I wanted another chance to be heard. I never felt like I got to during the criminal trial. I wanted to speak out against domestic abuse. In the spring of 2004, I called them about my case, and they agreed to represent me.

Tuesday May 31, 2005: the first day of the civil trial.

I was so nervous I was going to have to face my ex-husband again for the first time in three years. When I walked into the courtroom, Frank wouldn't stop staring at me. We sat only five feet from each other. When I looked at my ex-husband, I only saw evil. His eyes were piercing, narrowed slits that bore into my own eyes. I needed a glass wall—a barrier. The officer had strapped a belt around Frank's waist, so if he came after me or did anything crazy, the officer would push a button to send an electric charge that would drop him to the ground. Frank never tried. It was nerve-wracking to sit in the same space and breathe the same air. The court appearance was the first time I went somewhere without scar-covering makeup, making me feel naked and vulnerable. The attorneys thought the judge, jury, and Frank should see what I looked like underneath my protective foundation.

The first day was just motions, the information that would be allowed, or not allowed, to be presented during trial. It consumed the better part of the day, so we never called any jurors. I was alone except for my attorneys from the Never Again Foundation, Keith Perkins and Kent Phelps.

We weren't allowed to say the "Defendant Frank" or that Frank was incarcerated. The jurors never saw the security belt on his waist, and the jurors never knew that he had been on trial before for the same attack or of his previous convictions.

Frank had committed nearly an identical act on Jody, a girl he was with prior to meeting me. He'd been abusive and she was scared. She wanted to leave him and he held her at knife point. Our stories were nearly the same. He'd been convicted of it, but the judge had not allowed her to testify at my criminal trial Keith had spoken with Jody at length over the phone. He knew her story, its similarities to my own, and he knew we needed her for our case. This brave woman was willing to return to Arizona to testify, just as she'd been willing for the criminal trial. The judge wouldn't allow it. It was all Keith could do to contain himself. He maintained professionalism but his voice carried the weight of the urgency. He reminded the judge how critical it was that the jury knew the true history. My attack was not an isolated event. It was a pattern of behavior.

Both Keith and Kent were frustrated, dumbfounded, and angry. I thought it was wrong and unfair. I was confused. Why can't the jury know? I felt like the jury was made to assume that this was a marital issue and I was merely looking for financial compensation

Chapter Thirteen | Never Again

to appease emotional distress from past abuse. That's it. Like history repeating itself with the criminal trial. The Foundation's attorneys could never say Frank was, in fact, a felon, and currently serving time for aggravated assault. The jury was never allowed to know that I was not personally paying the attorneys, and that they were pro-bono attorneys from their own non-profit firm, who were paid solely from donations and grants. The jury, I thought, perceived me as a woman who could afford attorneys and was chasing more money. It wasn't the case at all. It was never about the money—it was the message.

By way of court-condoned character assassination, Frank, who represented himself, was allowed to talk about me being an exotic dancer. He was allowed to talk about my mom's old criminal charges. But we could not say that "the defendant" had been charged with aggravated assault in the past. We could not talk about any criminal charges on his record from the past ten years. Yet they could talk about anything concerning my mother and me from the last thirteen years. Frank used it to his advantage, telling the court I lied to an officer, about my last name, thirteen years ago during a traffic stop.

Just like in the criminal trial, it seemed that things were getting more unfair by the minute. I thought since it was a civil trial it would be different. I was wrong. Keith and Kent were beside themselves with frustration, but in a determined effort not to blow the case altogether, they kept themselves in check.

The judge behaved like he liked Frank and favored him. He would say how well he was doing for defending himself, and if he needed suits to wear, he had some in the back. Unbelievable!

We left about 1:00 p.m. I was just glad that it was over. I was tense all day. I would have to come back again on "day two" and see his face again.

The second day, Wednesday June 1, 2005, we were going to pick the jurors. There was one who had a mother that had been in prison before and her ex-boyfriend used to abuse her. We asked all the jurors different questions, like are they against dancers, or about their perceptions and experiences with domestic violence, or drug or alcohol abuse. Then we chose who we wanted and scratched those we didn't. We selected them out of thirty-five possible jurors. My ex-husband didn't scratch any so we pretty much got to pick who we wanted. We had an eight-panel jury made up of three men and five women. We chose some good jurors. But one, it turned out later, wasn't what we'd hoped because she didn't fully disclose personal truths.

We had eight people on the jury. After we picked the jurors, they came in the room and sat in the jury box while the others were excused. This was already the end of the second day. I had to come back the next day, "day three," and see my ex-husband again. It felt so bad sitting in the same room with him every day. I had so many different emotions, mad, sad, scared, and nervous. I'd look over at him to my right, past Kent and Keith. He'd always be staring at me. He had papers all layed out in front of him like he was trying to impress or intimidate me.

My feet were sweating, but I still felt in control. It was crazy. It was really hard to go to court every day. It was an hour's drive from my home and then I'd be there for eight hours.

It was summer in Arizona and school was out. My kids were staying home and they were getting into trouble while I was gone.

My son threw a rock and broke a neighbor's window. I was exhausted every day and twice during the first week of trial, I came home to find police at my house because Alex had done something. I would get home by 6:00 p.m. and deal with police, kids, and a messy house, then cook dinner try to spend time with Chelsea and Alex. Each night I'd write about the day's events, trying to vent my tension and fears. My day was usually not over until 11:00 p.m. I would have to get a suit ready for the next day, then go to sleep so I could get up for court. It was emotionally draining and nerve-

Chapter Thirteen | Never Again

wracking, and hard for the kids too. They didn't understand what was going on.

On the third day, Friday, we were going to start to call all the witnesses. Keith and Kent got everything ready. The first on the stand was Officer Spitler. He said the call he went on that night will never leave his mind. My lawyers asked him why and he said because the amount of blood. He'd never seen that much blood and he was the first officer to find my mother lying in the carport. He said he walked over to my mother and found that she was already dead. My lawyers continued to ask questions and he was on the stand for about an hour. Then Frank cross-examined the officer.

After that we called our next witness, Detective D'Angelo. My lawyers asked him to describe what he'd seen that day and showed pictures on a big screen asking, "Is this the room you saw that day?" Or "is this the kitchen you saw that day?" And so on. Then Frank started to cross-examine the detective. Frank had pictures too and he said, "This picture, the windows are shut and the blinds are closed, and the drawers on the dresser are shut." Then Frank pulled out the other picture and said, "Now, why Detective D'Angelo, is this drawer sticking out and the window open and the blinds open?" Frank said, "You guys were obviously moving things around and tampering with things." Detective D'Angelo said, "Well sir, we had to open drawers to look for stuff and we had to move things around to do our investigation." Frank, the defendant, was just trying to come up with as many things as he could think of to make the case look weak.

The next witness was scheduled to be Dr. Mosharrafa, my plastic surgeon. We expected him but he could not come that day. So we asked him if he could do a satellite interview during a break in his day. Dr. Mosharrafa agreed, so we told him we'd record later in the day and just bring it to the court. But Frank rejected that, "Well I could get just anybody as a witness and just record them." I think Frank was more concerned with what Dr. Mosharrafa would say.

We were going to try to get satellite for another day so we could still get his testimony. That way Frank could ask him questions too. Dr. Mosharrafa's testimony would be delayed until we were ready to record him on Monday, June 6th.

Our next witness was Dr. Keen, the medical examiner who did my mother's autopsy. He took the stand and my lawyers asked him, "How did Vina die?" "A stab wound to the neck." He explained specifically how the knife went in downward from neck to chest. The lawyers asked him how many autopsies he'd done in his career and he said over 20,000. My lawyers asked exactly how my mother died and he said that her heart filled with blood and that stopped her heart. "Did she have any other wounds?" "Yes, on her face, legs, and arms."

In his cross-examination, Frank asked Dr. Keen, "Is it possible she could've gotten stuck in the neck due to a struggle?" Dr. Keen said, "It is possible but very unlikely." Frank said, "No further questions." It was almost 4:00 p.m. and Dr. Keen was our last witness. We were going to return on Monday for Dr. Mosharrafa, and I was going to go on the stand. Frank would cross-examine me, could it be any worse? Then he would tell his side of the story. At last, the end of day three, June 2nd. I had Friday, Saturday, and Sunday to relax (OK try to relax) and get ready to testify.

Day Four, Monday June 6, 2005. This was the big day. I was going to have to go on the stand. Thankfully, I didn't have to go first and would have some time to compose myself. I got to court and they were getting all the equipment ready for Dr. Mosharrafa to testify through satellite. Once it was set up, we started with Dr. Mosharrafa's testimony. Frank didn't like the way the picture transmitted because it wasn't clear and the sound quality was poor. So he objected and said he could have anybody be a witness and nobody would know who it was on the other side. Everyone had to take a break while they tried to adjust the audio/visual so

Chapter Thirteen | Never Again

Frank would be happy. The technician went to his car and got more equipment and tried to make it better. We were ready to start again and the jurors came back in. We put Dr. Mosharrafa on the satellite, and Frank objected again to the picture and sound, but the judge overruled and let it go on. My lawyers asked Dr. Mosharrafa about all of my wounds and asked if they were life-threatening. Dr. Mosharrafa said the one on my neck was life-threatening because when you get stabbed on the scalp, you can bleed to death.

He explained how I'm going to have problems with my thumb for the rest of my life. There was not much more he could do about my thumb surgically. He described how he had to reattach my nose. Then Frank cross-examined him and he said to Dr. Mosharrafa, "So if I cut off my finger I will die of loss of blood?" Dr. Mosharrafa said, "No, that's not what I'm saying." "So how could she die of loss of blood?" Dr. Mosharrafa repeated, any time there is a scalp wound, you could bleed to death. Frank asked, "Did she get stabbed forty times?" Dr. Mosharrafa said, "It was around forty times." "Stabbed or slashed?" "Some were stab wounds and some were slashes." "No further questions." At last.

I was called to the stand. I took a deep breath and walked up. How can you anticipate and want something so much as your day in court, and still dread it?

Kent asked me his questions. Frank stood up to cross-examine me. He started by asking me things such as, "How was your relationship with your mom? Wasn't it true that you lied to the police officers before?" I reminded him, "Yes, I was young. It was fifteen years ago. I had expired tags and I gave them a fake name because I didn't want to go to jail." He said, "Have you ever hit me before, Tracy?" "No way." He knew that. Frank commented, "You're so innocent. You've never hit anyone in your life, huh?" I said, "That's not what I'm saying, I've hit people in my life. I just never hit *you*." Sarcastically, "Why am I so special?" "I never hit you because of your evil eyes." That's when he started to laugh. "Isn't it true you were real jealous over my relationship with my son?" **His** son! "Not at all, I would always want my kids close to their dad." There wasn't much left for Frank to ask because my lawyers and I got everything out before he got the chance. He really didn't know what to say. Frank saw that I was being very brave and he was not going to beat me down. I was going to win this one.

He tried several times to intimidate me and scare me. He would look at me with those evil eyes but I looked right back with confidence. I'd come a long way. I knew his games now and he was not going to run all over me. "I have no further questions," he resigned. It wasn't as bad as I thought it was going to be, I think because I was prepared.

Frank put himself on the stand and told his version of the story. He was talking in circles and not making sense. He said that my mom and I jumped on his back and he took the knife out of my mom's hand and went to punch me and her. He said he forgot he had the knife in his hand, and that's how we all got stabbed. He didn't explain anything about me being tortured for hours; he just did not have a story. He didn't know what to say so he started to cry in hopes I'd feel sorry for him and the jury would sympathize with him. But like I said, I know his games now. When he looked at me and said, "Why are you doing this Tracy? I loved you so much and I still love you to this day." Gazing at the ceiling, I ignored him.

Frustrated, he told the jurors, "I'm going to get custody of my son one way or another." He looked at me, "Whether you like it or not." Then he sat down and looked over at me and hissed just loud enough for me to hear, "You're a dead bitch." It wouldn't be on the court transcript and the jury didn't hear it. Just like he'd done at the criminal trial.

The judge would see him whispering to me but he didn't do anything about it. But my lawyers heard it. Kent tried his hardest

Chapter Thirteen | Never Again

to bring it to the judge's attention, getting up from his seat saying, "Your Honor, did you see that?" No apparent reaction from the judge and no admonishment to Frank. The judges always seemed to be on his side. I could see right through him, but everyone else gets manipulated by him, especially judges. Frank is very charming and people believe him. I did for a while and I've been through a lot because of it. I can usually read people well, but Frank is good at deception.

After Frank went on the stand, we had closing arguments. My lawyers got up there and told the whole story, showing pictures too, from beginning to end, but never mentioned Frank was a convict because they weren't allowed to. Kent did such a good job, and said it all just like it happened with all the police photographs. Frank got up for his closing remarks and cried and made no sense. Then, in a shift of attitude, he would get mad and say he was indigent and had no lawyers and this was all unfair. His mood swings would change minute to minute.

That was it for "day four." A huge relief. We'd gotten through it! The jurors were excused after instructions that we were going to reconvene at 9:00 a.m. on Tuesday, June 7th to hear the verdict. Kent and Keith assured me that I'd done a good job. They said I was confident and just told the story the way it was. I did get everything out I wanted to say, except all the things I was not allowed to mention. But I was allowed to say more during this trial than the criminal one four years earlier. So to me, I felt I'd won already. I had a second chance to be heard.

Tuesday, "day five," June 7, 2005, we came in and waited for a verdict. I thought they would have it by 10:00, or at least by lunch. We got there at 9:00 and sat and read and walked around the halls. I was restless and nervous. Frank was in a holding room. I would go to my car and make phone calls. It was blazing hot. Typical for Arizona in June. But I had to get out of the building. I called my son's doctor over and over because he was out of medication but he never returned my messages. I had been in trial almost two weeks and missed my son's appointment. He needed medication, but my hands were tied. Alex had been off Ritalin for a while and was out of control. All I did was walk or sit in the cafeteria and read my mail. I was basically roaming from 9:00 to 4:30, but they still didn't have a verdict. The day was wasted. The judge had us called back into the courtroom and told us we needed to go home for the day and come back again in the morning. Frank stood up and said he wanted to go back to the prison. That, of course, was his first reference to his place of residence, but of course, the jury wasn't in the room. Wednesday is when they transport them back and he wanted to be on that bus. He didn't want to stay another day for the verdict. He said, "I'm sure she won anyway and I just want to go home." The judge reminded him, "You'll give up your rights to be here if you leave." Frank understood. So we waited.

The sixth and last day of the civil trial was Wednesday, June 8, 2005. I didn't have to be there till 9:30; the others had to be there at 8:30 or 9:00. My lawyers told me to hang around; it would be all day or just a little while—no one could know for sure and verdicts were unpredictable. We sat in the cafeteria and ate a snack. I brought books to browse through. We wandered upstairs where another hearing was going on so we had to sit out in the hall. Keith and Kent brought their laptops and worked. I wished I had something to do.

We talked about custody. I asked, "What am I going to do now? Frank keeps talking about how he's going to get custody whether I "like it or not." I better start doing something, because he kept talking to the security guard while we were in the courtroom. Frank was telling him how he couldn't wait to get out so he could go back to his country. The security guard asked where that was and he said, "Panama." If he thinks he has plans to get Alex and take off to Panama, he's going to have a custody battle. My lawyers assured me

Chapter Thirteen | Never Again

they had lawyers that might help me. It gave me peace of mind.

It was 2:00 p.m. and we were still waiting. The jurors sent out a paper with two questions. The jurors asked, "How does this civil suit address the cycle of abuse?" My lawyers answered the question that once the message is out that violence is not tolerated it might stop the cycle of abuse. The next question was, "What has the defendant been convicted of and what is his sentence?" My lawyers answer by saying, "He was convicted of aggravated assault and kidnapping against Tracy." It's still so frustrating that my mother's death barely factors into it. Worst of all, Kent and Keith were prohibited from saying anything about Frank's previous girlfriend and the events that happened between the two of them. They could never say she'd been willing to testify that Frank had done virtually the same thing to her. It was information the jury needed to hear and needed to know. The jurors were real tough. They just kept asking questions and were taking forever to come up with a verdict. So we just waited again as the clock inched its way to 3:00 p.m.

At last, the bailiff came out and said the jury was ready. We all went in and they got the video camera set up. The jurors came in and the bailiff took the paper and read it expressionlessly before giving to the judge. He said, "For intentional infliction of emotional distress on Alex, we're in favor for the Plaintiff. And for negligent infliction of emotional distress we're in favor for the Plaintiff. For Alex, compensatory damages $50,000 and punitive damages $50,000, and for Tracy for assault and battery we're in favor for Plaintiff. For intentional infliction of emotional distress for Tracy, we favor for Plaintiff. And for wrongful death for Vina we favor for the Defendant. For false imprisonment on Tracy we favor for the Plaintiff. For compensatory damages we award $68,000. And for punitive damages we award $32,000 for Tracy."

I was really happy, but also really sad. The amount of money requested was something we had left open to the jurors to decide for us. The total amount was $200,000. It was alright. It would stick to Frank for a long time, maybe for life. But at the same time, I started to cry, because they favored for the wrongful death for the defendant, again, and I just couldn't understand that no one could see that he killed my mom. He *did*. And he keeps saying it's "self-defense" and everyone believes him! Even when we showed them a picture of me and one of my mother, they "favored" him. I had the same wound as my mother two centimeters above her wound. Two centimeters below her wound I had another just like it. Frank had tried to stab me the same way. I still can't see how anyone would believe a man has to attack a woman as violently as he did—in self-defense? It was so obvious that he killed my mom.

That day they called the verdict, I was very confused. I was happy they understood a little, but I was still crying for my mother. She still hasn't gotten justice. But I know, in spirit, she's happy for me. So I felt a gamut of emotions. My lawyers got to go in and talk to the jurors that wanted to stay and talk. There were five that stayed and three that left. I went to have a salad in the cafeteria because we weren't sure if the jurors would want to talk to me. After I made my salad, my lawyers called and said the jurors wanted to meet me. I went to the conference room and there were five of the jurors and my lawyers. I asked why they favored for the defendant in my mother's murder. They said they had to go with the juror's instructions and it said, "If the Defendant in his mind felt any kind of threat it *could be* self defense."

That means, if in his mind, he really believed she was going to hurt him, he had to go after her first, because he feared her. It gives the defendant, one who's convincing and persuasive, a real open door to claim self-defense. The jurors said they didn't know if my mother really came after him, or what really happened, so that's why they did what they did. I asked, "Why so little money?" Under Arizona civil law, the jury doesn't have to be unanimous, but they have to be nearly so. In an eight-panel jury like ours, six could

Chapter Thirteen | Never Again

agree and two could dissent. In our case, three had dissented. They said they wanted to give a lot more for punitive damages. One juror wanted to give me $11 million. But a woman on the panel believed that "God would take care of it in the afterlife," the five remaining jurors told us, and that had swayed the other two. She'd said, "There is no need for money. What good is that going to do? Get her nails done?" Keith, Kent, and I were surprised, and angry, to learn that this juror had been a victim of abuse, to some degree, in her marriage. She had never revealed it when all jurors were asked, point blank, during the selection process, if they or a family member had ever been exposed to domestic abuse.

In return, the jury was surprised to learn about us. They had no idea it wasn't about the money, since we weren't allowed to tell them during court. We weren't allowed to tell them my lawyers were from the Never Again Foundation, and they were doing this for free through donations and grants. These attorneys never earn fees from jury awards. They help women who have been wronged by the justice system involving domestic violence. They help women go after offenders in civil court and sue for pain and suffering to make abusers pay for what they've done, instead of getting away with murder like my ex-husband did.

The jurors had no idea. They were stunned when they found out. The Never Again Foundation is the first in the country of its kind. I guess they just thought I was a money-hungry lady that could pay for lawyers so I could get rich off my ex. Why wouldn't they think that since I wasn't allowed to tell them anything? We also weren't supposed to say anything about my ex-husband being in prison. They had absolutely no idea he was currently in prison for what he'd done. These are some of the things I can't understand about the "justice" system. But we finally got to tell the jurors the whole truth off the record. I think they felt badly. I could see it in their faces. I could see tears in their eyes. We got to tell them everything now that the trial was over. So we talked about anything we wanted. They got to see what we were really about, and about the Foundation. As we talked to them, my lawyers kept getting phone calls from reporters, both from TV news and newspapers. My lawyers asked the jurors if they were willing to talk to some reporters and a few said they would. Alone again, I went back to finish my salad. Then I joined the others outside.

In front of the courthouse, the *Arizona Republic* was talking to jurors, writing quick notes, and interviewing my lawyers. When the reporter was done with my lawyers, he came over to me and was asking me how I felt about the verdict and everything that had happened. He also had the newspaper articles from four years earlier when the attack happened. The videographer wanted to interview me on camera. For the next five minutes, he talked with me, asking how I felt. Two Phoenix channels, 3 and 12, interviewed the jurors and talked to my lawyers. Keith and Kent explained how they were from the Never Again Foundation and the jurors admitted they really wanted to give me more but one juror didn't. It was a constant battle so they had to settle for what they could get with this other juror. Clearly the jurors who were in support of me in terms of my fight against abuse, and the award they wanted to give, were the ones that remained. There's a wonderful piece of news footage where one of the female jurors explained that they wanted to give me more money but they couldn't get a consensus. What was important to them was to send the message that abuse is not OK and not tolerated.

When the reporters finished their jury interviews, they came back over to me. We sat on a bench under a small tree. Blessed shade! I sat there on camera and spoke with them for half an hour. They asked how our marriage was and why I left Frank. I told them the whole story and told them how much time he got for murdering my mom and slashing and stabbing me. They just could not believe it. I told them I had sued him civilly because I wanted justice to be served. I wanted him to pay one way or another. With

Chapter Thirteen | Never Again

this lawsuit, he would have to pay for the rest of his life. If he got a job, even one in prison, paying me would be his form of life sentence, which he should have gotten in the criminal trial. His wages would always be attached. Then they asked what I thought about the verdict I said I wished that they would have found him guilty of my mom's murder. I wished they gave me more money, but $200,000 should make him suffer for awhile when he gets out. I felt justice was finally served and I felt I was able to be heard a little more in the civil suit. I still couldn't say certain things but I was allowed to say a little more this time than the near nothing in the criminal trial. That was one of the main reasons I did this suit. I would have a chance at a fair trial, so I could say more of what happened. They finished interviewing me and they had me walk into the courthouse so they could videotape me and told me it would air at 4:00 and 10:00 p.m. The reporters left wishing me good luck.

I hugged Kent and Keith goodbye. We'd been down a long road together. I was crying for many reasons. I was sad that my mom still didn't get sympathy, or justice, and I was happy and thankful for my lawyers and everything they'd done for me. It was an emotional time. I just had so much in my head. I thought I was going to have a nervous breakdown. I hugged everyone and thanked them. When I got home, I watched the news, and all I could see was how bright the scar was on my face. It made me extremely self-conscious. I will have to see these scars for the rest of my life and I hope my ex will have to pay for the rest of his.

The dictionary's definition of serrated is: "having or denoting a jagged edge." And so describes my life. It has had false starts and progress. It has had ups and downs. I keep thinking I'm finally getting ahead to a normal life and there's another setback. I have lived my life on the edge. I've had moments of joy and times of despair. Back and forth like a saw—or a cutting knife.

EPILOGUE

For the last few years, I have been getting blood work checked every six months and there is still no sign of Hepatitis C. I feel so lucky. I was so happy I got rid of a deadly disease so I could grow old with my children. After I completed treatment, I started to grow my hair back, I recovered from the injection bruising on my stomach and legs, and things got back on track in my life. My children and I survived this crazy ordeal and we were going to get things right again. I started to go back to school and just lived on Social Security Income. I joined a grief support group, a Hepatitis C support group, and domestic violence support groups to share my story. I met a lot of women just like me. Then I joined the Arizona Coalition Against Domestic Violence. I volunteered as a mentor to try to help other women in my situation. I volunteered to do public speaking on domestic violence. I spoke at the governor's office and in different cities and in hospitals and churches and I even spoke in front of about twenty domestic violence convicts. I appeared on the Montel Williams show. I was very nervous to tell my story to the whole world, and as I walked onto the stage I thought I was going to faint. Then he started to ask me questions and all the horrified feelings came back and I started to cry. But I did great considering how nervous I was and seeing all the bloody photos Montel put on the big screen. What killed me the most was talking about my son.

It's been nine years since the attack. I'm going to school and taking my son to counseling and psychiatrists. He's still on medication and has anger problems. He once killed a bird. He throws rocks at houses and breaks windows. Because of that we've had to move a few times and change schools. He is very friendly to people and very smart, but he's a nervous wreck and hyperactive. I have problems with him at school, recreational programs, and summer programs. Everyone complains about him and cannot handle him. I have to tell the schools what he'd been through and I didn't know what to do and I didn't want to put him on medication. After being sent home all the time from school for behavior problems and getting suspended, I told the psychiatrist what was going on. He told me he needs medication for the post traumatic stress disorder and ADHD. He said things would change if I just put him on medication. So at this point I had no choice. We started medication and everyone everywhere; principals, teachers, etc. could tell the difference. They all said he was concentrating more and listening and he was more focused. But there were days I'd forget to give him the medication and the school would call me right away and ask me if he'd had his pill. I would say, "No I forgot" so they would send him home. I have to give him medication just to make everyone else happy. I just hope he grows out of all this behavior.

As for my daughter, she is an A student and on the principal's list. But she is a little depressed and sleeps a lot. She will not talk to anyone. Her grandmother was her best friend. She seems really mad at me. I think she blames me for the whole attack. I'm still trying to be her friend and work on our relationship.

In 2004, I received my GED, general equivalency diploma, two decades after I would have graduated high school. I wanted to work with abused women, like social work, but I finally decided to go to school to become a registered nurse because I can work in several different areas in the field: shelters, schools, and drug rehab.

My goal is to open a shelter for victims of domestic abuse. In memory of my mother, I want to call it "Vina's Place." I will be the Executive Director so that I can oversee all the things I believe a shelter should have. And based on my past experience where nursing care wasn't available when I needed it, I will be the on-site nurse. A portion of the profits from this book will help attain that goal.

I'm confused about the future. Would I ever marry again? Would I get over the scars on my face? What will happen when Frank's out of prison? I feel scared and alone, just me and the kids. I'm trying to get through nursing school the best I can so my kids and I will have a good future. I date once in a while, but I really don't think about having a boyfriend or husband. The desire is gone, I'm happy by myself. I know I could use help from time to time and would like a companion, but I'm pretty content with my life. I am a nervous wreck sometimes; I go through spells of depression. My children and I are all alone, but all I want in life is to get through school and buy a house. I have been working really hard on writing this book with Stephanie to share my story. She is a very special and caring person, and if it were not for her this book would have never happened. I thank her with all my heart.

My life has been one thing after the other. I live on SSI. I've been more settled in recent years. No homelessness. I can relax a little. I still live check to check. I don't have the luxury of spending money. But we get by. I get $1,300 a month from SSI for myself and the two kids. The ironic thing is, in the state of Arizona the current cost to house an inmate, like Frank, for one month is over $1,800. He's still getting more than me.

People want to judge by what little they know and what they see. Both the criminal and civil trials proved that to me. "She's a stripper, you know." "Oh." As if that explained everything. They don't know the abandonment and loneliness. They don't know the kid I was who searched for food. They don't know the woman who scrubs her toilets and dusts meticulously. They haven't seen the flowers and religious symbols decorating the house. They haven't asked me about my desire for education and the dreams I had of a mutually committed marriage raising children to be happy, healthy members of the community.

Until I complete my nursing degree, I'm grateful for the Social Security Income; it's the only thing I can depend on, and it will be there until I can get us by on my own.

I have overcome thoughts of suicide, guilt, and deep, deep depression. But most importantly, I'm a child of God who is no longer a victim, but a champion of hope and life. The emotional scars are the hardest to deal with and God can heal us inside never-the-less. We have moved on and I survived. Finally.

MY HERO
3/18/05

The person I picked have changed a lot of peoples life. My hero is my mother not only because she has been there for me its because of the hero she is today for surviving what has happened to her what happened to her was trajic and will never leave my family or me again. In 2001 my mom nearly died she was stabbed 40 times and my grandma died how this incident happened was her ex-husband got and at her and went crazy. Got out the knife and started stabbing my mom sliced my grandmas throat. My grandma got out of the house buy only made it halfway to the neighbors house to get help and died in the middle of the road while my mother thought my grandma was getting help my mom was still getting stabbed while he was stabbing her suddenly the knife broke on her shoulder so my mom thought it was all over but it wasn't, he got out the sissors and used those to stab her with them finally he stopped and got the phone and called his mother which called my nana which called the police my moms ex then started stabbing my mom again the police didn't get to the house intill another 5 hours then they got there and they took her to the hospital and my mom found out what had happened to my grandma but my mom didn't tell me intill another 2 weeks after all this stuff happened my mom didn't know how to tell me because me and my grandma did everything together in till that day. All I want to do is go back and erase everything. While all of this was going on I had spent the night at my friends house so I was at my friends house that day but unfortianitly my brother which is now 5 years old saw every thing so he now has to take meds. Not only did my moms ex hurt my mom physically but also emotionally and luckily he did not hurt my brother physically but did hurt him emotionally. My moms ex only got 12 years in prison for killing my grandma and stabbing my mom 40 times my mom also hopes when he get out he does not look for her and kill her. Today she goes around allover to speak about what has happened to her to teach girls to be very carefull. We also pray but we still have the memories.

by Chelsea, Tracy's daughter, at age 12
(reproduced exactly as written)

ARE THESE THINGS HAPPENING IN YOUR RELATIONSHIP?

Physical Abuse
Your partner ...
- breaks things
- slaps or punches you
- shoves you
- bites you
- chokes you
- hurts your children

Verbal and Emotional Abuse
Your Partner ...
- calls you stupid or worthless
- becomes extremely jealous of family and friends
- has a temper that frightens you
- says, "I did it for you own good"
- calls you dirty names

Sexual Abuse
Your Partner...
- accuses you of being unfaithful
- will be pacified if you give in
- forces you to do things you don't want to do sexually

Abuse through Control
Your Partner...
- controls the money
- tells you what to wear
- monitors your whereabouts at all times
- questions your parenting skills
- criticizes you in front of the children
- belittles your family and friends

If you feel:
- Afraid to tell others what is happening at home
- It is all your fault.
- You were wrong and somehow provoked the abuser.
- The abuser should be forgiven because of abuse of alcohol or drugs.
- No one else would want you.

These are all signs of an abusive relationship. If you are experiencing these types of issues in your relationship you are not alone! Source: AZVictims.com

REFERENCES AND RESOURCES

National Network to
End Domestic Violence...................................www.nnedv.org

Battered Women's Justice Project ....www.bwjp.org

National Coalition Against
Domestic Violence   ....www.ncadv.org

Office for Victims of Crime .... www.ojp.usdoj.gov/ovc

Never Again Foundation .... www.neveragainfoundation.org

The A.C.E Study..www.acestudy.org

Heath After Trauma...................www.healthaftertrauma.com/

SUGGESTED READING

The Stalking of Kristen (1995), Lardner Jr., G. The Atlantic Monthly Press, New York

To be an Anchor in the Storm (1997), Brewster, S., Ballantine Books, New York

Next Time She'll be Dead – Battering and How to Stop it (1994), Jones, A., Becon Press, Boston

Not To People Like Us- Hidden Abuse in Upscale Marriages (2000),Weitzman, Ph.D., S., Basic Books

Why Does He Do That? - Inside the Minds of Angry and Controlling Men (2002) Bancroft, L., G.P. Putnam and Sons, New York

The Physician's Guide to Intimate Partner Violence and Abuse, A reference for all health care professionals (2006) Salber, M.D., P. and Taliaferro, M.D., E, Volcano Press. Volcano, CA

ABOUT THE AUTHORS

STEPHANIE ANGELO

No stranger to family abuse from her own past life, Stephanie Angelo is an award winning consultant and trainer who pioneered a proprietary financial model to determine the impact of domestic abuse on businesses; having a positive ripple effect to every corner of the company.

From executive boardrooms to prisons, and from victims to offenders, Stephanie speaks and consults nationally to organizations, conferences and coalitions. Her first book, Bringing the Darkness into the Light, provides stories of survival along with vital resources and safety information.

TRACY STOMBRES

Tracy Stombres is a single mother of two, a nursing student, and a public speaker on domestic violence. Prior to becoming a student to finish nursing school, she spent the past ten years as Medical Assistant and Nursing Assistant for a women's clinic and a nursing homes. She is at a turning point in her life and has overcome many obstacles. Tracy is seeking creative ways to open a domestic violence shelter in her mother's name; Vina's Place. She is excited to help other women who suffer domestic violence. She is an active, well rounded individual with promising career ahead of her.